Moving On

BEGINNING LISTENING

BOOK 2

Jann Huizenga

photographs by Van Bucher

Longman

Moving On: Beginning Listening Book 2

Longman Inc., 95 Church Street, White Plains, N.Y. 10601

Associated companies:
Longman Group Ltd., London
Longman Cheshire Pty., Melbourne
Longman Paul Pty., Auckland
Copp Clark Pitman, Toronto
Pitman Publishing Inc., New York

Executive Editor: Joanne Dresner
Development Editor: Penny Laporte
Text Designer: Lynn Luchetti, Pencil Point Studio
Cover Designer: Stephan Zander
Photographer: Van Bucher
Illustrators: Pencil Point Studio, Ray Skibinski

Library of Congress Cataloging-in-Publication Data

Huizenga, Jann.
    Moving on / Jann Huizenga.
        p.   cm. – (Beginning listening : bk.2)
    ISBN 0-8013-0119-X
    1. English language–Textbooks for foreign speakers.
2. Listening–Problems, exercises, etc. I. Title. II. Series:
Huizenga, Jann. Beginning Listening : bk. 2.
PE1128.H784 1989   8839644
428.3′4–dc19   CIP

89 90 91 92 93 9 8 7 6 5 4 3 2

Distributed in the United Kingdom by Longman
Group Ltd., Longman House, Burnt Mill, Harlow,
Essex CM20 2JE, England, and by associated
companies, branches and representatives
throughout the world.

Printed in the U.S.A.

CONTENTS

INTRODUCTION

Moving On is a photograph-based listening comprehension text intended for students who have had little exposure to spoken or written English.

The material has been written with several goals in mind. One is to provide students with truly "comprehensible input", i.e., an acquisition stage in which a high degree of contextualization would allow them to formulate hypotheses and discover meaning in language they are hearing for the first time. Thus the workbook and tape include a presentation stage in which the new language on tape is contextualized not only by its situational authenticity but by its exact correspondence with a series of photographs in the student's book. The extra-linguistic context is seen as crucial in helping students at this level to understand and acquire. Another goal of the material is to give students ample opportunity to test their new hypotheses. Therefore, the *Focus* exercises are designed to allow students to verify their comprehension in a simple, non-verbal fashion. Finally, the material aims to give students a chance to listen to language and absorb it before producing it. Production is thus delayed until the end of each unit, where optional production activities can be found.

Each of the 10 units begins with a brief, contextualized dialogue establishing the setting and associated language or functions. Early units, for example, introduce quantities in the context of a supermarket (*some/any*), a post office (*how much/two 25-cent stamps*), or a farmer's market (*four pounds*). Later units present functions such as requesting information or making complaints. As students listen to the conversation on tape, they follow along in the workbook with a series of photographs representing the phrases they are hearing. In the *Focus* section, students receive feedback on their comprehension through tasks in which they respond non-verbally, by circling, numbering, checking, matching, or drawing. They then progress to recognition of written forms. For students who are ready to produce, the *Follow Up* section at the end of each unit provides oral and written production tasks.

USING THE TEXT

Before playing the presentation on tape, give your students a minute to look at the overview photo, which will make the general setting clear, and then at the rest of the photos, which will clarify the particular topics. Briefly previewing in this manner will allow students to predict what is coming and thus to relax and better comprehend. The presentation occurs twice on the tape, the first time with the narrator interjecting the numbers of the photos to assure that students make the correct correspondence between language utterance and photo. The second time is without the narrator. If your students want to listen again, rewind and play the tape as many times as necessary. The *Focus* section consists of five or six listening tasks, all requiring non-verbal responses to recorded material. The first provides feedback to students on how well they have understood and internalized the language in the presentation. The next introduces students to the written form of what they have heard. The following tasks allow students to test their comprehension of the language in a recombined form. The *More New Words* exercise expands on the Presentation by introducing additional vocabulary. Students may need to listen to an exercise more than once. Each exercise should be checked immediately after it is completed since the exercises build upon each other. A good way to do this is to elicit answers from students and then replay the exercise once or twice. This will allow students with incorrect answers to better understand the source of their errors. An answer key is found at the back of the text. The optional *Follow Up* activities require production and are not on tape. These exercises provide communicative, cooperative-learning tasks for students who are ready to produce. For the first exercise, students work in pairs: one looking at the unit page, the other looking at the page in the Appendix. After completing the task, the students verify the accuracy of the exchange by looking at each other's page. The second exercise is a life-skills writing task.

ACKNOWLEDGMENTS

Special thanks to photographer and friend Van Bucher for his professionalism, patience, and unflagging cheerfulness throughout this long project. Thanks also to my husband Kim Crowley, who helped and put up with everything, and to family and friends who so gamely agreed to be photographed. At Longman, Penny Laporte, Development Editor, spent long hours poring over a complicated manuscript and never failed to come up with creative suggestions and solutions to problems. This text owes much to her expertise. Executive Editor Joanne Dresner's guidance at all stages was also invaluable in shaping this book.

Look at the pictures and listen.

1.

2.

3.

4.

5.

6.

7.

8.

9.

one   1

FOCUS

Exercise 1

Listen to the conversations. Match the conversations with the pictures.

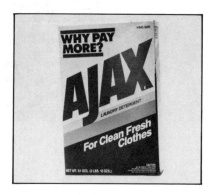

a. _____

b. _____

c. _____

d. ___|___

e. _____

f. _____

g. _____

h. _____

Exercise 2

Number the sentences as you hear them.

a. _____ Anything else?

b. _____ Excuse me, where is the cooking oil?

c. _____ Laundry detergent?

d. _____ They're in aisle 4.

e. __1__ Do we need flour?

f. _____ And the cookies?

g. __2__ Yes, we're almost out.

h. _____ Oh! We need milk and eggs.

i. _____ Yeah, we don't have any.

j. _____ It's in aisle 3.

k. _____ Yes, we need a loaf of bread and some cereal.

Exercise 3

Listen and circle the words you hear.

1. bread
   milk
   eggs
   cereal

2. cookies
   milk
   cereal
   cooking oil

3. cereal
   flour
   bread
   eggs

4. laundry detergent
   milk
   cereal
   flour

5. bread
   cookies
   oil
   flour

6. eggs
   cookies
   detergent
   cereal

Exercise 4   More New Words

Look at the pictures and listen.

noodles

a. aisle _____4_____

rice

b. aisle _____

toilet paper

c. aisle _____

hot dogs

d. aisle _____

tea

e. aisle _____

peanuts

f. aisle _____

Now listen again and write the aisle number.

Exercise 5

Listen and circle the verb you hear.

1. is   (are)

2. is   are

3. is   are

4. is   are

5. is   are

6. is   are

Exercise 6

Listen and check (✔) the items you hear in each conversation.

	1.	2.	3.	4.	5.
a.					
b.					
c.					
d.					
e.					
f.					
g.					
h.	✔				
i.					
j.					
k.	✔				
l.					

FOLLOW UP

Exercise 7

Work with a partner.

One student is the shopper and looks at this shopping list.
The other student is the stockperson and looks at page 69.

The shopper asks where items are. The stockperson gives the aisle number.
The shopper writes the number on the shopping list.

Look at each other's page and make sure the aisle numbers are correct.

Then change roles.

SHOPPER: Where's the flour?
STOCKPERSON: It's in aisle 2.

SHOPPER: Where are the hot dogs?
STOCKPERSON: They're in aisle 1.

Shopping List	
flour	2
hot dogs	1
noodles	___
nuts	___
toilet paper	___
corn flakes	___
bread	___
eggs	___
rice	___
tea	___
milk	___
laundry detergent	___
cookies	

Exercise 8

Coffee was spilled on this shopping list.
Write the missing letters.

shopping list

Corn fl
tea
laundry dete
Italian bre
hot dog
toilet
flou
cooki
peanu

Unit 2

How much is this first class?

Look at the pictures and listen.

1.

2.

3.

4.

5.

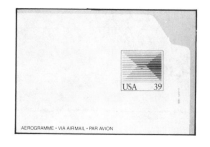

6.

7.

FOCUS

Exercise 1

Listen and circle the item you hear.

a.	b.	c.	d.

1.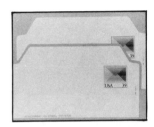

2.

3.

4.

21902	20912	20902	20903

5.

6.

1•17 +	2•17 +	2•17 +	1•17 +
0•50 +	0•50 +	0•60 +	0•60 +
0•65 +	0•65 +	0•65 +	0•65 +
0•25 +	0•25 +	0•25 +	0•25 +
2•57 *	3•57 *	3•67 *	2•67 *

Exercise 2

Number the sentences as you hear them.

a. __2__ First class? Let's see. You need 65¢ on it.

b. _____ Yes. One aerogramme, please.

c. __1__ How much is this first class?

d. _____ I'd also like six 25-cent stamps and one 15-cent stamp.

e. _____ Anything else?

f. _____ And don't forget the zip code.

g. _____ Here you are. Altogether that's $4.49.

h. _____ And this letter is airmail.

i. _____ Oh, sorry. It's 02139.

j. _____ OK. Airmail to Venezuela is 45¢.

Exercise 3

Can you predict what the clerk will say?
Listen and circle the response.

1. a. It's 14625.
   b. A 15-cent stamp.
   c. You need $1.25 on it.

2. a. OK. Anything else?
   b. Two stamps.
   c. Airmail?

3. a. One?
   b. OK. Airmail to France is 45¢.
   c. It's 11101.

4. a. That's 75¢.
   b. First class.
   c. Three aerogrammes.

5. a. OK. That's 25¢.
   b. OK. That's 45¢.
   c. OK. That's 90¢.

Exercise 4   More New Words

Look at the pictures and listen.

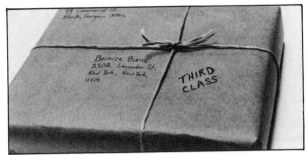

1.
a package

That's __$3.00__ .

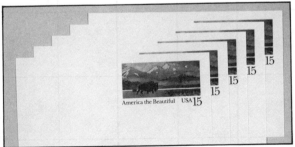

2.
a book of stamps

That's _____ .

3.
a money order

That's _____ .

4.
postcards

That's _____ .

Now listen again and write the price.

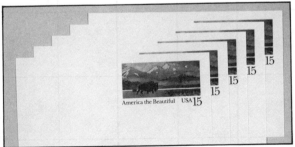

Exercise 5

Listen and check (✔) the items you hear in each conversation.
Write how many of each item the customer wants.

		1.		2.		3.		4.	
		✓	How many?	✓	How many?	✓	How many?	✓	How many?
a.	15¢ OLIVER WENDELL HOLMES	✓	3						
b.	USA 20¢	✓	2						
c.	USA 25 Jack London								
d.	Samuel P. Langley Aviation Pioneer 45 USAirmail								
e.	TWENTY $5.00 STAMPS								
f.		✓	2						
g.									
h.	CUSTOMER'S RECEIPT	✓	1						

FOLLOW UP

Exercise 6

Work with a partner.

One student is the clerk and looks at this page.
The other student is the customer and looks at page 70.

The customer asks to buy or mail each item on the page.
The clerk writes how many items the customer wants.
Then the clerk adds up the prices and gives the total.

Look at each other's page and make sure the amounts are correct.

Then change roles.

CUSTOMER: I'd like six 25-cent stamps.
CLERK: Anything else?
CUSTOMER: How much is this package third class?
CLERK: $1.50. Is that it?

How Many?		Price
_____	15-cent stamp(s)	_____
_____	25-cent stamp(s)	_____
_____	45-cent stamp(s)	_____
_____	50-cent stamp(s)	_____
_____	aerogramme(s), 39¢ each	_____
_____	postcard(s), 15¢ each	_____
_____	money order, add 75-cent charge	_____
_____	book of stamps	_____
_____	package, $1.50 third class	_____
	TOTAL	_____

Four pounds of apples, please.

1.

Look at the pictures and listen.

2.

3.

4.

5.

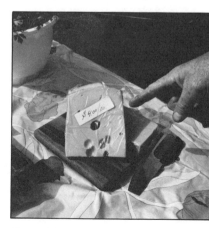

6.

7.

FOCUS

Exercise 1

Listen and circle the items you hear.
Note: *lb. = pound*

a.

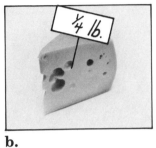

b.

c.

d.

e.

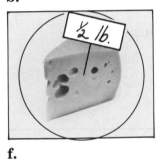

f.

g.

Exercise 2

Listen and circle the items you hear.

a.

b.

c.

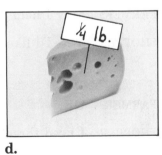

d.

e.

f.

g.

Exercise 3

Number the sentences as you hear them.

a. _____ Four dollars a pound.

b. _____ All right. Give me a quarter of a pound.

c. __1__ May I help you?

d. _____ No, that's all.

e. _____ How much is it?

f. _____ OK. What else?

g. __2__ Yes, I'd like a pound and a half of onions.

h. _____ Some cheese.

i. _____ Anything else?

Exercise 4

Complete the conversation.

pounds   head   cheese   apples   half   bunch

FARMER: May I help you?

SHOPPER: Yes, I'd like a _____*head*_____ of lettuce and
          ₁

          a _____ of radishes.
                ₂

FARMER: OK.

SHOPPER: I need three _____ of potatoes, too.
                        ₃

FARMER: What else?

SHOPPER: Two pounds of _____ .
                        ₄

FARMER: Anything else?

SHOPPER: How much is the _____ ?
                        ₅

FARMER: $4.25 a pound.

SHOPPER: OK. Give me _____ a pound.
                    ₆

Exercise 5   More New Words

Look at the pictures and listen.

bananas

a. ___2___

tomatoes

b. _____

strawberries

c. _____

eggs

d. _____

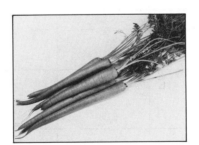

carrots

e. _____

beans

f. _____

Now listen again and match the words with the pictures.

1. a dozen   4. a half a pound of

2. a pound of   5. a bunch of

3. a box of   6. two pounds of

Exercise 6

Listen and write how much of each item the customer wants.
Use these words: *pound(s), head(s), dozen, bunch(es), box(es).*

		1.	2.	3.	4.	5.
a.		¼ pound				
b.						
c.						
d.						
e.						
f.						
g.						
h.						
i.						
j.						
k.		1 box				
l.						

FOLLOW UP

Exercise 7

Work with a partner.

One student is the farmer and looks at this page.
The other student is the shopper and looks at page 71.

The shopper circles the items and the amount of each item
he/she wants to buy and tells the farmer.
The farmer circles the items and the amount.

Look at each other's page and make sure the circled items and the amounts
are correct. Then change roles.

SHOPPER: Two pounds of potatoes, please.
FARMER: Anything else?
SHOPPER: Yes, I'd like a dozen eggs and a bunch of radishes.
FARMER: OK. What else?

½ 1 2 3 4 5 lb(s). ½ 1 2 3 4 5 lb(s). ½ 1 2 3 4 5 lb(s). ½ 1 2 3 4 5 lb(s).

½ 1 2 3 4 5 lb(s). ½ 1 2 3 4 5 lb(s). ½ 1 2 3 4 5 lb(s). 1 2 3 4 5 head(s)

1 2 3 4 5 bunch(es) 1 2 3 4 5 dozen 1 2 3 4 5 box(es) 1 2 3 4 5 bunch(es)

Exercise 8

Complete the shopping list.

half a pound of cheese   a bunch of bananas
two pounds of apples   a pound of onions
a dozen eggs   a bunch of carrots
a head of lettuce   three pounds of potatoes

Farmer's Market

a dozen eggs _____

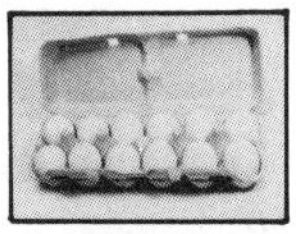

_____   1 lb.

_____

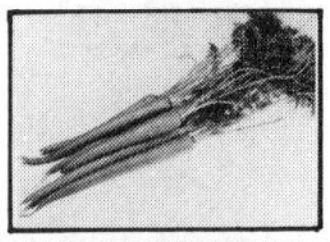

_____   3 lbs.

_____

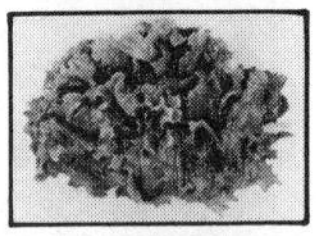

_____   ½ lb.

_____

_____   2 lbs.

Do you have white semi-gloss paint?

Look at the pictures and listen.

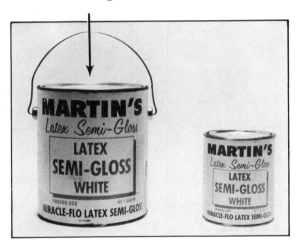

1.

2.

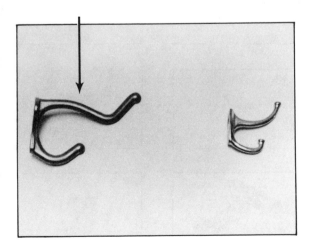

3.

4.

FOCUS

Exercise 1

Listen and circle each item the customer wants.

	a.	b.	c.	d.
1.			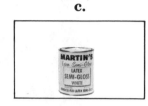	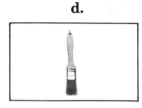
2.				
3.				
4.			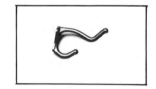	
5.				
6.			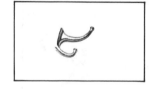	
7.				

Exercise 2

Number the sentences as you hear them.

a. __2__   Here it is. Do you need a paintbrush?

b. _____   Fine. Oh, and I need a few hooks.

c. __1__   I need a gallon of white semi-gloss paint.

d. _____   Large. I'll take two.

e. _____   All right. How's this?

f. _____   Yes, actually, I do.

g. _____   Over here. We have all sizes. Large? Small?

h. _____   Narrow.

i. _____   We have many sizes. Wide or narrow?

j. _____   Oh, excuse me. I need some batteries, too.

Exercise 3

Listen and check (✔) the words you hear.

1. _____ quart
   __✓__ paint
   _____ wide
   __✓__ paintbrush

2. _____ quarts
   _____ hooks
   _____ small
   _____ sizes

3. _____ paint
   _____ two
   _____ small
   _____ batteries

4. _____ quart
   _____ wide
   _____ paintbrush
   _____ paint

5. _____ narrow
   _____ quart
   _____ batteries
   _____ small

6. _____ wide
   _____ large
   _____ white
   _____ hooks

Exercise 4   More New Words

Look at the pictures and listen.

1.

screws

a. _____

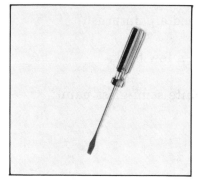

screwdriver

b. _____

masking tape

c. _____

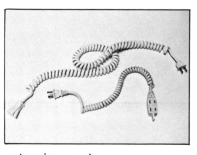

2.

extension cords

a. _____

hammer

b. _____

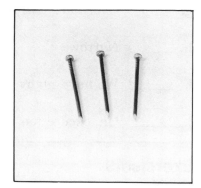

nails

c. _____

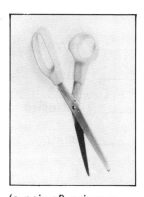

3.

(a pair of) scissors

a. _____

lightbulbs

b. _____

a 60-watt bulb

c. _____

a 100-watt bulb

d. _____

Now listen again and number the words as you hear them.

Exercise 5

Listen and check (✓) the items each customer wants.
Circle the size of the items.

		1.		2.		3.		4.
a.		quart gallon		quart gallon		quart gallon		quart gallon
b.		small large		small large		small large		small large
c.	✓							
d.								
e.		wide narrow		wide narrow		wide narrow		wide narrow
f.	✓	6 feet ⟨10 feet⟩ 12 feet		6 feet 10 feet 12 feet		6 feet 10 feet 12 feet		6 feet 10 feet 12 feet
g.		60 watt 100 watt		60 watt 100 watt		60 watt 100 watt		60 watt 100 watt
h.								
i.								
j.		small large		small large		small large		small large
k.	✓	narrow ⟨wide⟩		narrow wide		narrow wide		narrow wide

FOLLOW UP

Exercise 6

Work with a partner.

One student is the salesperson and looks at this page. The other student is the shopper and looks at page 72.

The shopper circles the items he/she wants to buy and tells the salesperson. The salesperson circles the items.

Look at each other's page and make sure the circled items are correct.

Then change roles.

SHOPPER:	I need a gallon of paint.
SALESPERSON:	All right.
SHOPPER:	And a wide paintbrush.
SALESPERSON:	Anything else?
SHOPPER:	Yes, I need some screws and a screwdriver.

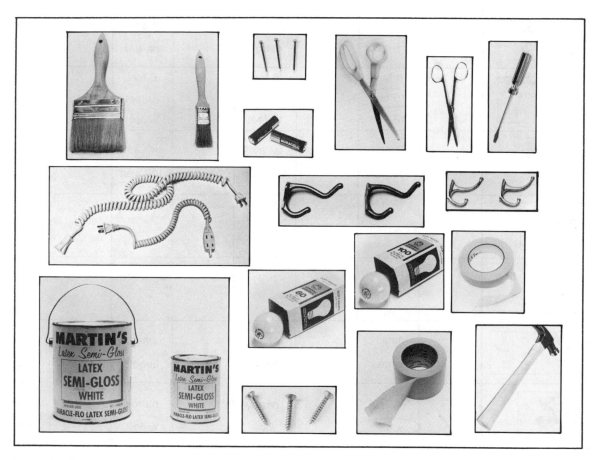

Exercise 7

There are several mistakes in this ad. Read the ad and correct them.

HEFTY HARDWARE [SALE!!]

Batteries
49¢ for 2
60 and 100 watt only

Hooks
99¢ each

Paintbrushes
Semi-gloss
$6.99/gallon
10 colors

MARTIN'S
LATEX
SEMI-GLOSS
WHITE

Screws
Only $1.49 for 2
Any size

Do you want
a ride home?

Look at the pictures and listen.

1.

3.

4.

5.

6.

FOCUS

Exercise 1

Listen and circle the picture that matches what you hear.

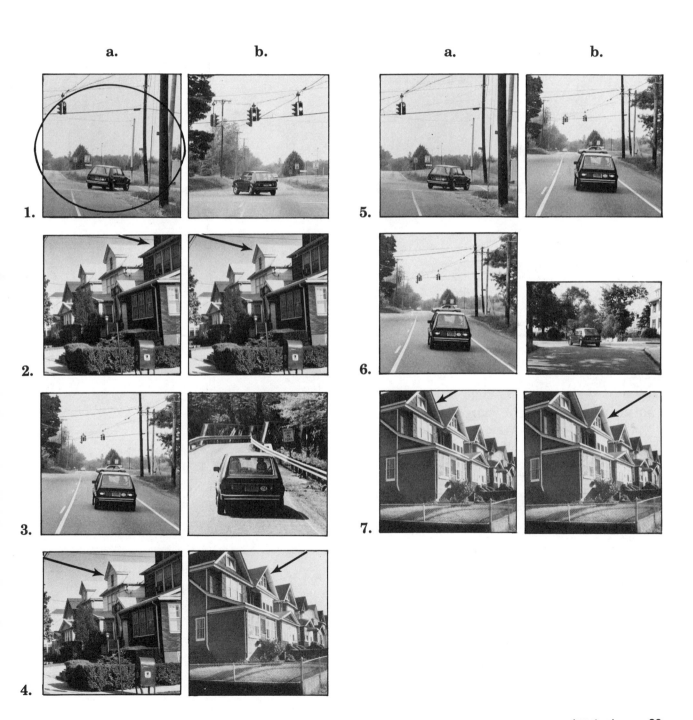

Exercise 2

Number the sentences as you hear them.

a. _____ Now how do I get to your place?

b. _____ Go straight to the light. Then turn left.

c. _____ It's the second house on the left.

d. __/__ Do you want a ride home, Paul?

e. __2__ Yeah, sure. Thanks.

f. _____ At the light?

g. _____ Uh-huh. Go over the bridge and turn right at the first intersection.

h. _____ Yeah. left.

i. _____ Straight?

j. _____ OK.

Exercise 3

Listen and circle the words you hear.

1. a. Go / straight / right
    b. (Go / straight / light)
    c. Go / second / light

2. a. Make / left / first / intersection
    b. Make / left / first / bridge
    c. Make / left / second / intersection

3. a. first / left / bridge
    b. first / house / bridge
    c. first / house / left

4. a. second / house / right
    b. second / house / left
    c. second / house / light

5. a. Turn / right / straight / light
    b. Turn / right / second / light
    c. Turn / right / first / light

Exercise 4   More New Words

Look at the map and listen.

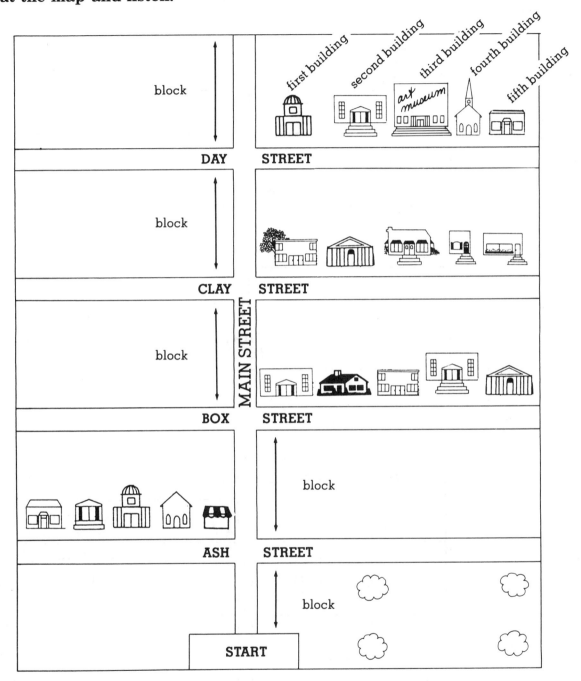

Now listen again and write these names on the map.

1. art museum
2. bank
3. bus station
4. library
5. post office

Exercise 5

Listen to the conversations. Find the house or apartment building and circle it.

KEY
- • light
- ⌂ house
- ▯ apartment building

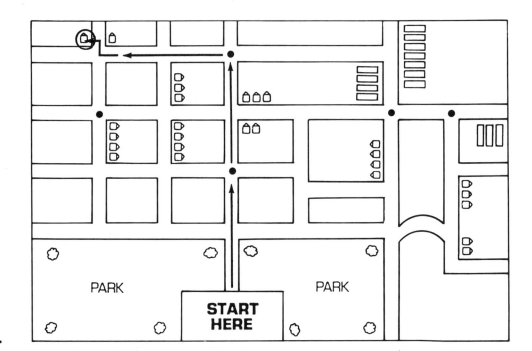

1.

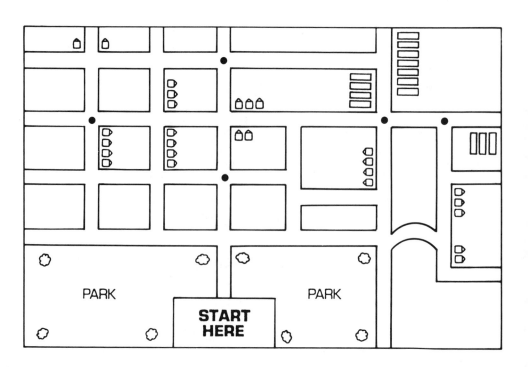

2.

3.

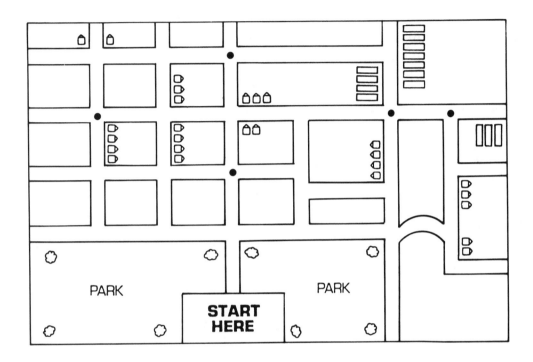

4.

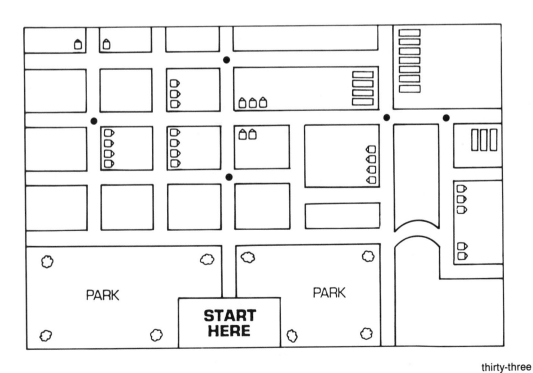

FOLLOW UP

Exercise 6

Work with a partner.

One student looks at this map, circles a house or apartment building on the map, and then gives directions to this place.

The other student looks at the map on page 73, finds the place, and circles it.

Look at each other's page and make sure the same place is circled.

Then change roles.

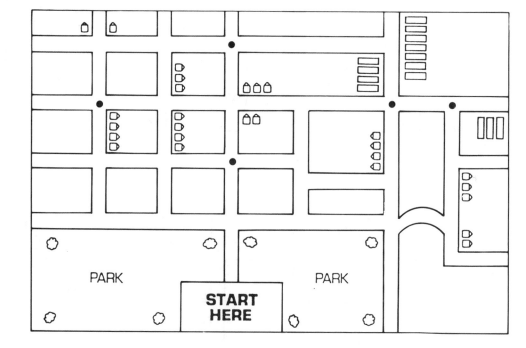

KEY
- light
- house
- apartment building

Exercise 7

Complete the directions.

straight	left	right	blocks
fifth	second	turn	

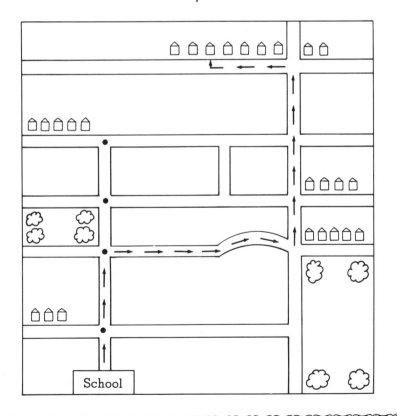

Come to a PARTY!!

Place *Sarah Mills, 88 Brian Rd.*

Date *May 20*

Time *4:00 – 8:00*

Directions: From school, go _____*straight*_____ to
                                        1
the _____ light. Turn _____. Go
          2   3
over the bridge and turn _____. Go
                                 4
three _____ and _____ left at the
          5   6
intersection. It's the _____ house on the right.
                              7

> What time is the next train to White Plains?

Look at the pictures and listen.

Leave	Arrive
New York	North White Plains
PM	PM
1:00	1:48
1:30L	2:22
1:48E	2:26
2:00	2:48
2:30L	3:22
2:48E	3:26

1.

Leave	Arrive
New York	North White Plains
PM	PM
1:00	1:48
1:30L	2:22
1:48E	2:26
2:00	2:48
2:30L	3:22
2:48E	3:26

2.

3.

```
SEPT. 8          WHITE PLAINS

Ⓜ Metro-North    SUBJECT TO
  Commuter       TARIFF        Ⓜ
  Railroad       REGULATIONS

$3.75    GRAND CENTRAL TERMINAL

SEPT. 8 GRAND CENTRAL TERMINAL

Ⓜ Metro-North    SUBJECT TO
  Commuter       TARIFF        Ⓜ
  Railroad       REGULATIONS

$3.75            WHITE PLAINS
```

4.

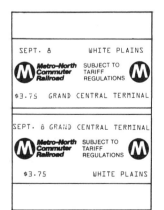

5.

Ⓜ **Metro-North Commuter Railroad**
PASSENGER'S RECEIPT
Received of Holly Jay
(Passenger's Signature)
$ 7.50   in payment for
transportation ticket issued
From New York / White Plains
To White Plains / New York
This receipt is for payment for the ticket
and will not be accepted for credit or refund
on your monthly commutation ticket.

THANK YOU! WE'RE GLAD TO
HAVE YOU ABOARD

AGENT STAMP HERE

SEP -8
WHITE PLAINS,
N.Y.

6.

7.

FOCUS

Exercise 1

Listen to the conversations. Circle the pictures that match what you hear.

	a.	b.	c.	d.	e.
1.					
2.					
3.					
4.					
5.					
6.					

Exercise 2

Number the sentences as you hear them.

a. _____ When does it arrive?

b. _____ A round-trip ticket to White Plains, please.

c. __1__ What time is the next train to White Plains?

d. _____ Window 11.

e. _____ OK. Here you are. It leaves from Track 25.

f. _____ Is it local or express?

g. _____ 3:22.

h. __2__ There's one at 2:30.

i. _____ Local.

j. _____ Where do I buy a ticket?

Exercise 3

Can you predict what the clerk will say? Listen and circle the response.

1. a. (Window 7.)
   b. A round-trip ticket.
   c. Track 7.

2. a. Track 12.
   b. That's $8.50.
   c. Over there.

3. a. At 3:30.
   b. Express.
   c. Window 3.

4. a. At window 3.
   b. At 3:00.
   c. Track 3.

5. a. Over there. Window 2.
   b. It leaves from Track 2.
   c. It arrives at 12:30.

6. a. OK. Here you are.
   b. That's $10.75.
   c. One way.

Exercise 4   More New Words

Look at the schedule and listen to a part of each conversation.

New York – Boston Trains	
DAILY	
Departures	Arrivals
6:00 AM	10:00 AM
9:13 AM	12:30 PM Express
1:20 PM	5:05 PM
4:55 PM	

1.

Midwest Air Chicago – Detroit Schedule	
DAILY (WEEKDAYS)	
Departures	Arrivals
5:18 AM	6:10 AM
8:00 AM	8:50 AM
	2:30 PM

2.

Washington – Philadelphia Buses	
DAILY	
Departures	Arrivals
6:45 AM	8:30 AM
10:04 AM	12:15 PM
3:08 PM	

3.

Now listen again and complete the schedules.

Exercise 5

Listen and write the information you hear.

	1.	2.	3.	4.	5.
a.	5				
b.	$7.50				
c.	15				
d. (Arrivals)					
e. (Departures)	2:30				
f.	Round Trip				

FOLLOW UP

Exercise 6

Work with a partner.

One student looks at the schedule on this page. The other student looks at the schedule on page 74.

Ask each other for the missing information on your schedules. Fill in your schedules with the information.

Then look at each other's page and make sure the information is correct.

STUDENT A: What time is the next train to Boston?
STUDENT B: There's one at 9:05.

STUDENT B: When does it arrive?
STUDENT A: It arrives at 1:00 P.M.

STUDENT A: Where do I catch it?
STUDENT B: Track 12.

Destination	Departure Time	Arrival Time	Track
BOSTON	9:05 AM	1:00 PM	12
PHILADELPHIA	9:42 AM	12:35 PM	6
WASHINGTON			14
NEWARK	10:49 AM	11:30 AM	2
CONCORD		2:54 PM	
NEW HAVEN	12:02 PM	1:42 PM	7
PORTLAND	12:30 PM	4:59 PM	9
NEW BRUNSWICK	1:20 PM		15
CHICAGO	1:33 PM	10:00 PM	1
PRINCETON		3:17 PM	11

Exercise 7

Complete the note.

arrives   9:20   round-trip
tickets   express   track

6-18

Holly,

I bought our __tickets__ .
1

We leave tomorrow at 9:40

from _____ 8. I think it
2

_____ at 12:30. (It's
3

_____) I'll meet you at
4

the information booth at

_____ — OK?
5

Love,

Linda

P.S. The _____ ticket
6

is $11.50.

1.

Look at the pictures and listen.

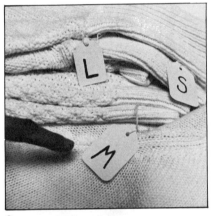

2.

3.

4.

5.

6.

FOCUS

Exercise 1

Listen to the conversations. Circle the picture that matches what you hear.

a.	b.	c.

1.

2.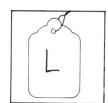

3.

4.

5.

6.

Exercise 2

Number the sentences as you hear them.

a. __2__ Sure. What size do you need?

b. _____ How much is it?

c. _____ The dressing rooms are over there.

d. _____ Oh, that's nice. Where can I try it on?

e. __1__ Can I see that sweater? The white one in the window?

f. _____ Oh, probably a medium.

g. _____ They run small, medium, and large.

h. _____ How about this?

i. _____ It's on sale for $12.

j. _____ I'm also looking for a black cotton skirt, size 10.

Exercise 3

Can you predict what the clerk will say? Listen and circle the response.

1. a. The dressing rooms are over there.
   b. (Sure. What size do you need?)
   c. How about this?

2. a. Oh, probably medium.
   b. They run small, medium, and large.
   c. It's on sale for $30.

3. a. $25.
   b. A black skirt.
   c. Only large.

4. a. The dressing rooms are over there.
   b. What size do you need?
   c. It's on sale for $15.

5. a. How about this?
   b. Probably small.
   c. Size 12.

6. a. Medium.
   b. Yes, for $10.
   c. A white sweater.

Exercise 4　　More New Words

Look at the pictures and listen.

1.
jacket

  a. I don't really like the style.
  b. (Probably large.)
  c. It's too long.

2.
blouse

  a. No, it's not.
  b. Probably a medium.
  c. Yes, that's nice. How much is it?

3.
pants

  a. What's your size?
  b. The dressing rooms are over there.
  c. How about these?

4.
(striped) shirt

  a. It's on sale for $15.50.
  b. Large.
  c. They run small, medium, and large.

5.
(leather) gloves

  a. No, they're too small.
  b. Probably a medium.
  c. Where can I try them on?

Can you predict what the people will say? Listen again and circle the response.

Exercise 5

Listen and number the pictures as you hear them.

1.

a. __1__

b. __2__

c. __3__

2.

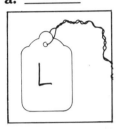

a. _____

b. _____

c. _____

3.

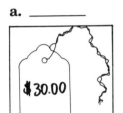

a. _____

b. _____

c. _____

4.

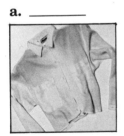

a. _____

b. _____

c. _____

5.

a. _____

b. _____

c. _____

FOLLOW UP

Exercise 6

Work with a partner.

One student is the shopper and looks at this page. The other student is the salesperson and looks at page 75.

The shopper circles the items he/she wants to buy, and the sizes. Then the shopper talks to the salesperson.

The salesperson circles the items and the size, and tells the price. The shopper writes the price of the item.

Look at each other's page and make sure the information is correct.

Then change roles.

<table>
<tr><td colspan="7">Note on Clothing Sizes
Clothing can be small, medium, or large.
It can also be sold by size. For example:</td></tr>
<tr><td colspan="7">Women's</td></tr>
<tr><td colspan="7">blouses, jackets, pants, skirts, sweaters</td></tr>
<tr><td>U.S.</td><td>4</td><td>6</td><td>8</td><td>10</td><td>12</td><td>14</td></tr>
<tr><td>Metric</td><td>36</td><td>38</td><td>40</td><td>42</td><td>44</td><td>46</td></tr>
<tr><td colspan="7">Men's</td></tr>
<tr><td colspan="7">shirts</td></tr>
<tr><td>U.S.</td><td>14</td><td>14½</td><td>15</td><td>15½</td><td>16</td><td>16½</td></tr>
<tr><td>Metric</td><td>36</td><td>37</td><td>38</td><td>39</td><td>40</td><td>41</td></tr>
<tr><td colspan="7">pants</td></tr>
<tr><td>U.S.</td><td>30</td><td>32</td><td>34</td><td>36</td><td>38</td><td>40 (waist)</td></tr>
<tr><td></td><td colspan="2">short</td><td colspan="2">medium</td><td>long</td><td>(length)</td></tr>
<tr><td>Metric</td><td>46</td><td>48</td><td>50</td><td>52</td><td>54</td><td>56</td></tr>
</table>

SHOPPER: I'm looking for some black pants.
SALESPERSON OK. What size do you take?
SHOPPER: Probably a 38 long.
SALESPERSON: How about these? They're on sale for $12.99.
SHOPPER: Can I try them on?

4 6 8 10 12 14

$ _____

14 14½ 15 15½ 16 16½

$ _____

4 6 8 10 12 14

$ _____

S   M   L

$ _____

30 32 34 36 38 40
short   medium   long

$ _____

S   M   L

$ _____

Exercise 7

There are several mistakes in this ad. Read the ad and correct them.

MARTY'S SPORTSWEAR

SUMMER SALE!

Sizes: small, medium, and large

Beautiful white pants on sale now for **only $20.**

Black sweaters now **only $12.** Small sizes only.

Skirts in all sizes **on sale** for $15.

Are you busy right now?

Look at the pictures and listen.

1.

2.

3.

4.

5.

6.

FOCUS

Exercise 1

Listen to the conversations. Match the conversations with the pictures.

a. _____

b. _____

c. _____

d. _____

e. ___l___

f. _____

Exercise 2

Number the sentences as you hear them.

a. _____ Insert the paper tray like this.

b. _____ Turn it on here.

c. _____ How many copies do you want?

d. _____ Seven.

e. _____ Now press the start button.

f. _1_ Excuse me, Sara. Can you show me how to use this machine?

g. _2_ Sure.

h. _____ Then put your paper here, face down.

i. _____ OK. Press 7.

j. _____ Then turn off the machine.

Exercise 3

Complete the conversations.

on   copies   press
put   paper   off

WOMAN: Excuse me. Are you busy right now?

MAN: Not really. What do you need?

WOMAN: How do you use this machine? I need 10 ___*copies*___ .
1

MAN: OK. Turn it _____ here. Then insert the _____ tray,
2   3

like this. _____ your paper here. _____ 10. Now press
4   5

start. When you finish, turn _____ the machine. OK?
6

WOMAN: OK. Thanks a lot.

MAN: Anytime.

Exercise 4 More New Words

Look at the schedule and listen to a part of the conversation.

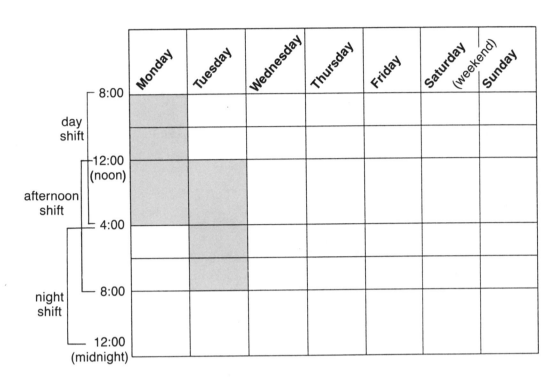

Now listen again and complete the schedule.

Exercise 5

Can you predict what the person will say?
Listen and circle the response.

1. a. Thanks.
   b. Excuse me.
   c. No, I'm sorry. I'm busy.

2. a. Oh, that's all right.
   b. Sure. Like this.
   c. Can you come in at 10:00?

3. a. Anytime.
   b. Fine.
   c. I see.

4. a. Turn it on here.
   b. Not really.
   c. I have class on Saturday.

5. a. Sure. Turn it on here.
   b. Turn off the machine.
   c. Then put your paper here.

6. a. Thanks for your help.
   b. I have class on Monday.
   c. 12:00 to 8:00? OK.

FOLLOW UP

Exercise 6

Work with a partner.

One student is the employee and looks at this page. The other student is the boss and fills in the schedule on page 76.

The employee asks questions about the schedule and the boss answers the questions. The employee fills in the schedule on this page.

Look at each other's page and make sure the schedules are the same.

Then change roles.

EMPLOYEE: What's my schedule for next week?
BOSS: You'll work the day shift on Monday and Tuesday. And the afternoon shift, noon to eight, on Wednesday, Thursday, and Friday.
EMPLOYEE: OK. Thanks.

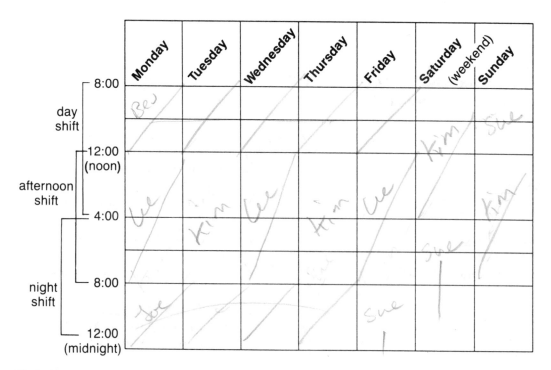

Exercise 7
Complete the instructions.

copies   turn   down
press   insert   put
on

COPIER INSTRUCTIONS

1. _Insert_ _____ the paper tray.

2. Turn the machine _____.

3. _____ the paper on the glass
   face _____.

4. Press the number of _____ you want.

5. _____ the start button.

6. _____ off the machine when you
   finish.

Unit

9

What seems to be the matter?

Look at the pictures and listen.

1.

2.

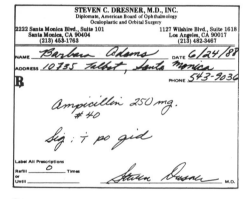

STEVEN C. DRESNER, M.D., INC.
Diplomate, American Board of Ophthalmology
Oculoplastic and Orbital Surgery

2222 Santa Monica Blvd., Suite 101   1127 Wilshire Blvd., Suite 1618
Santa Monica, CA 90404   Los Angeles, CA 90017
(213) 453-1763   (213) 482-3467

NAME *Barbara Adams*   DATE *6/24/88*
ADDRESS *10735 Talbot, Santa Monica*
℞   PHONE *543-9036*

Ampicillin 250 mg.
 # 40

Sig: ɨ po qid

Label All Prescriptions
Refill ___*0*___ Times
or
Until ___   *Steven Dresner* M.D.

3.

4.

5.

6.

Exercise 1

Listen to the conversations. Match the conversations with the pictures.

a. ___/___

b. _____

c. _____

d. _____

e. _____

f. _____

Exercise 2

Number the sentences as you hear them.

a. __2__ I have this bad cold.

b. _____ Let's take your temperature.

c. _____ I've got a terrible stomachache. I think it's the flu.

d. _____ Let me write you a prescription.

e. _____ Well, doctor, I have a very bad headache and a fever.

f. _____ I hope you'll feel better.

g. __1__ Hello. Ms. Adams? Come on in. What seems to be the matter?

h. _____ And I have this bad cough, too.

i. _____ Hello, Ms. Frank. What can I do for you?

j. _____ Hi, Mr. King. What's the matter?

Exercise 3

Listen and check (✓) the sentence you hear.

1. _____ **a.** You've got a fever.
   ✓ **b.** You've got the flu.
   _____ **c.** I've got the flu.

2. _____ **a.** I have a bad cold.
   _____ **b.** I have a bad cough.
   _____ **c.** I have a terrible cold.

3. _____ **a.** I have a very bad headache.
   _____ **b.** I have a terrible headache.
   _____ **c.** I have a terrible stomachache.

4. _____ **a.** I've got a headache and a fever.
   _____ **b.** I've got a cough and a fever.
   _____ **c.** I've got a fever.

5. _____ **a.** Let me take your temperature.
   _____ **b.** Let me write you a prescription.
   _____ **c.** Let's take a look.

Exercise 4   More New Words

Look at the pictures and listen.

1.    

earache   sore throat

_____|_____   _____

2.       

leg and foot   backache   neck

_____   _____   _____

Now listen again and number the words as you hear them.

Exercise 5

Number the parts of the body as you hear them.

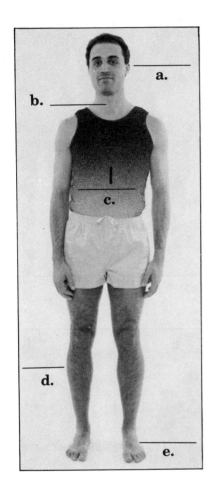

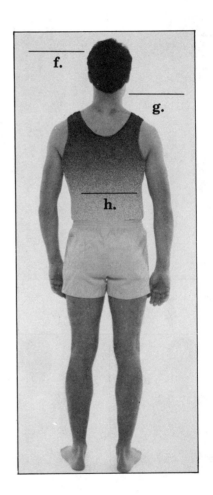

Exercise 6

Listen and check (✓) what is wrong with the person in each conversation.

1.

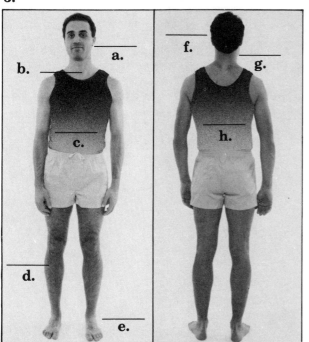

2.

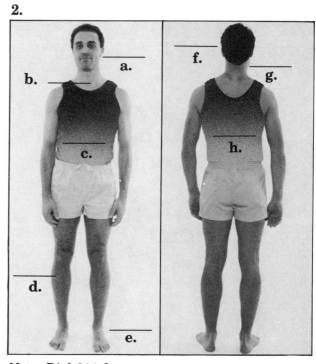

Note: Dial 911 for an emergency.

3.

4.

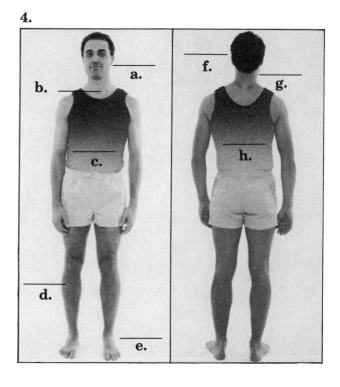

FOLLOW UP

Exercise 7

Work with a partner.

One student is the doctor and looks at this page. The other student is the patient and looks at page 77.

The patient checks (✓) what is wrong with him/her. Then the patient tells the doctor.

The doctor checks (✓) what is wrong and asks questions.

Look at each other's page and make sure they are the same. Then change roles.

PATIENT: Doctor, I have a very bad cough and a terrible sore throat.
DOCTOR: Do you have any fever?
PATIENT: No, I don't think so.

_____

_____

_____

_____

_____

_____

_____

_____

_____

_____

Exercise 8

Complete these notes using the following words:

earache   cough   sore

fever   foot

1.

APRIL 9

DEAR MR. WHITE,
JANE WILL NOT BE
IN SCHOOL TODAY. SHE
HURT HER _____.
SINCERELY,
MRS. WOO

2.

Dear Ms. Parks,   Feb. 6
Jose has a fever and
a _____ throat. He will
not be in school today.
Sincerely,
Mr. M. Perez

3.

Dr. Ellen Lawler
22 Broadway
New York, NY 10011

July 2

Iris Mott has a
_____ of 102° and
a bad _____. She
should stay in bed for
3 days.
Dr. E. Lawler

4.

March 26
Dear Miss Sanchez,
Paul is sick today.
He has an _____ and a
stomachache. Please excuse him
from school. Thank you.
Mr. Hold

Mr. Meyers,
we've got
problems!

Look at the pictures and listen.

1.

2.

3.

4.

5.

6.

FOCUS

Exercise 1

Listen to the conversations. Match the conversations with the pictures.

a. _____

b. _____

c. _____

d. _____

e. __/__

f. _____

Exercise 2

Number the sentences as you hear them.

a. _____ Look! The lock is broken.

b. _____ Yeah. I'll take care of it.

c. __/__ Mr. Meyers, we've got problems!

d. _____ The paint in here is peeling, too.

e. __2__ What's wrong?

f. _____ And the faucet leaks.

g. _____ The kitchen window is cracked.

h. _____ And in the bathroom, the bathtub is clogged.

i. _____ Let's see.

j. _____ And this outlet doesn't work.

Exercise 3   More New Words

Look at the picture and listen.

Now listen again and complete the sentences.

1. The light fixture _____
   a. leaks.
   b. is cracked.
   c. (is broken.)

2. The intercom _____
   a. doesn't work.
   b. is clogged.
   c. leaks.

3. The mirror _____
   a. is peeling.
   b. is cracked.
   c. is clogged.

4. The radiator _____
   a. leaks.
   b. is plugged up.
   c. is peeling.

5. The toilet _____
   a. doesn't work.
   b. is cracked.
   c. leaks.

6. The sink _____
   a. leaks.
   b. is plugged up.
   c. is cracked.

Exercise 4

Listen and check (✓) the items you hear in each conversation.

		1.	2.	3.
a.				
b.				
c.				
d.		✓		
e.		✓		
f.				
g.				
h.				
i.				
j.		✓		

FOLLOW UP

Exercise 5

Work with a partner.

One student is the tenant and looks at this page. The other student is the landlord and looks at page 78.

The tenant draws the problems in the apartment and then tells the landlord about them. The landlord draws each problem.

Look at each other's page and make sure they are the same.

Then change roles.

TENANT: We've got problems.
LANDLORD: What's the matter?
TENANT: The lock is broken, the radiator leaks, and . . .
LANDLORD: I'll take care of it tomorrow.

Exercise 6
Complete the letter.

window	paint	faucet
bathtub	leaks	outlet

13 Fox Road
Apt. 18
Los Angeles, CA   90035
March 21, 1990

Mr. Joel Meyers
Meyers Rental Agency
45 First Avenue
Los Angeles, CA   90035

Dear Mr. Meyers:

   We need some work done in our apartment. The
___paint___ in the kitchen and bathroom is peeling.
The bathroom _____ leaks and the _____
is plugged up. In the living room, the _____
is cracked, and the _____ doesn't work.
Sometimes the radiator _____.
   Would you please take care of these problems
as soon as possible? Thank you very much.

                          Sincerely,

                          Peggy Swain
                          Peggy Swain

APPENDIX

FOLLOW UP

Exercise 7

Work with a partner.

One student is the shopper and looks at page 6.
The other student is the stockperson and looks at this page.

The shopper asks where items are. The stockperson gives the aisle number.
The shopper writes the number on the shopping list.

Look at each other's page and make sure the aisle numbers are correct.

Then change roles.

SHOPPER: Where's the flour?
STOCKPERSON: It's in aisle 2.

SHOPPER: Where are the hot dogs?
STOCKPERSON: They're in aisle 1.

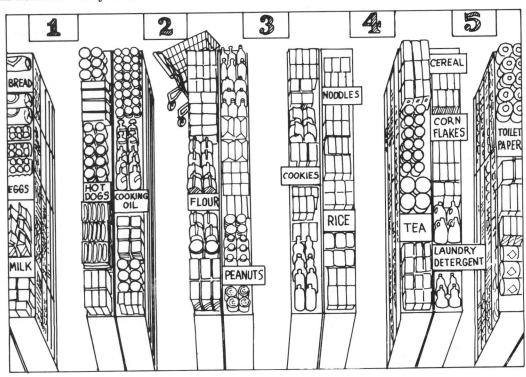

Exercise 6

Work with a partner.

One student is the clerk and looks at page 13.
The other student is the customer and looks at this page.

The customer asks to buy or mail each item on the page.
The clerk writes how many items the customer wants.
Then the clerk adds up the prices and gives the total.

Look at each other's page and make sure the amounts are correct.

Then change roles.

CUSTOMER: I'd like six 25-cent stamps.
CLERK: Anything else?
CUSTOMER: How much is this package third class?
CLERK: $1.50. Is that it?

 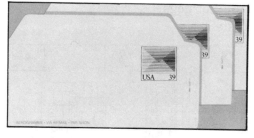 

FOLLOW UP

Exercise 7

Work with a partner.

One student is the farmer and looks at page 19.
The other student is the shopper and looks at this page.

The shopper circles the items and the amount of each item
he/she wants to buy and tells the farmer.
The farmer circles the items and the amount.

Look at each other's page and make sure the circled items and the amounts
are correct. Then change roles.

SHOPPER: Two pounds of potatoes, please.
FARMER: Anything else?
SHOPPER: Yes, I'd like a dozen eggs and a bunch of radishes.
FARMER: OK. What else?

½ 1 2 3 4 5 lb(s).	½ 1 2 3 4 5 lb(s).	½ 1 2 3 4 5 lb(s).	½ 1 2 3 4 5 lb(s).
½ 1 2 3 4 5 lb(s).	½ 1 2 3 4 5 lb(s).	½ 1 2 3 4 5 lb(s).	1 2 3 4 5 head(s)
1 2 3 4 5 bunch(es)	1 2 3 4 5 dozen	1 2 3 4 5 box(es)	1 2 3 4 5 bunch(es)

FOLLOW UP

Exercise 6

Work with a partner.

One student is the salesperson and looks at page 26. The other student is the shopper and looks at this page.

The shopper circles the items he/she wants to buy and tells the salesperson. The salesperson circles the items.

Look at each other's pages and make sure the circled items are correct.

Then change roles.

SHOPPER:	I need a gallon of paint.
SALESPERSON:	All right.
SHOPPER:	And a wide paintbrush.
SALESPERSON:	Anything else?
SHOPPER:	Yes, I need some screws and a screwdriver.

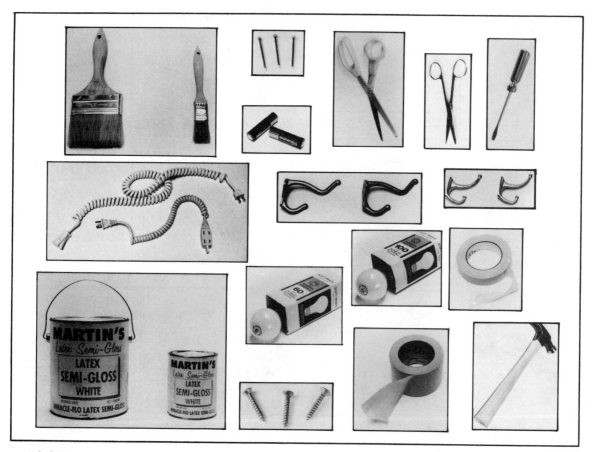

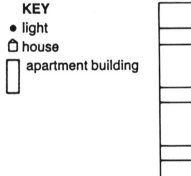

Unit 5 FOLLOW UP

Exercise 6

Work with a partner.

One student looks at the map on page 34, circles a house or building on the map, and then gives directions to this place.

The other student looks at the map, finds the place, and circles it.

Look at each other's page and make sure the same place is circled.

Then change roles.

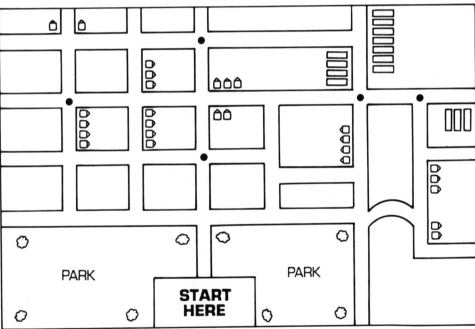

Exercise 6

Work with a partner.

One student looks at the schedule on this page. The other student looks at the schedule on page 41.

Ask each other for the missing information on your schedules. Fill in your schedules with the information.

Then look at each other's page and make sure the information is correct.

STUDENT A: What time is the next train to Boston?
STUDENT B: There's one at 9:05.

STUDENT B: When does it arrive?
STUDENT A: It arrives at 1:00 P.M.

STUDENT A: Where do I catch it?
STUDENT B: Track 12.

Destination	Departure Time	Arrival Time	Track
BOSTON	9:05 AM	1:00 PM	12
PHILADELPHIA			6
WASHINGTON	10:08 AM	2:20 PM	14
NEWARK		11:30 AM	
CONCORD	11:19 AM	2:54 PM	3
NEW HAVEN	12:02 PM		7
PORTLAND		4:59 PM	
NEW BRUNSWICK	1:20 PM	2:07 PM	15
CHICAGO	1:33 PM		1
PRINCETON	2:15 PM	3:17 PM	11

Exercise 6

Work with a partner.

One student is the shopper and looks at page 48. The other student is the salesperson and looks at this page.

The shopper circles the items he/she wants to buy, and the sizes. Then the shopper talks to the salesperson.

The salesperson circles the items and the size, and tells the price. The shopper writes the price of the item.

Look at each other's page and make sure the information is correct.

Then change roles.

SHOPPER:	I'm looking for some black pants.
SALESPERSON:	OK. What size do you take?
SHOPPER:	Probably a 38 long.
SALESPERSON:	How about these? They're on sale for $12.99.
SHOPPER:	Can I try them on?

Note on Clothing Sizes
Clothing can be *small, medium,* or *large.* It can also be sold by size. For example:

Women's

blouses, jackets, pants, skirts, sweaters

U.S.	4	6	8	10	12	14
Metric	36	38	40	42	44	46

Men's

shirts

U.S.	14	14½	15	15½	16	16½
Metric	36	37	38	39	40	41

pants

U.S.	30	32	34	36	38	40 (waist)
	short		medium		long	(length)
Metric	46	48	50	52	54	56

4 6 8 10 12 14

$25.00

14 14½ 15 15½ 16 16½

$~~13.99~~
$10.99

4 6 8 10 12 14

$40.00

S   M   L

$~~30.00~~
$20.00

30 32 34 36 38 40
short   medium   long

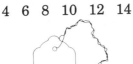

$~~15.00~~
$12.99

S   M   L

$30.00

FOLLOW UP

Exercise 6

Work with a partner.

One student is the employee and looks at page 54. The other student is the boss and fills in the schedule on this page.

The employee asks questions about the schedule and the boss answers the questions. The employee fills in his/her schedule.

Look at each other's page and make sure the schedules are the same.

Then change roles.

EMPLOYEE: What's my schedule for next week?

BOSS: You'll work the day shift on Monday and Tuesday. And the afternoon shift, noon to eight, on Wednesday, Thursday, and Friday.

EMPLOYEE: OK. Thanks.

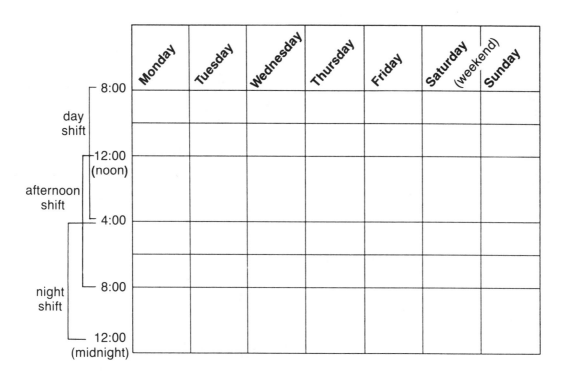

Exercise 7

Work with a partner.

One student is the doctor and looks at page 61. The other student is the patient and looks at this page.

The patient checks (✔) what is wrong with him/her. Then the patient tells the doctor. The doctor checks (✔) what is wrong and asks questions.

Look at each other's page and make sure they are the same. Then change roles.

PATIENT: Doctor, I have a very bad cough and a terrible sore throat.
DOCTOR: Do you have any fever?
PATIENT: No, I don't think so.

_____ _____ _____ _____

 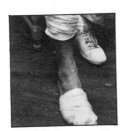  

_____ _____ _____ _____

_____ _____

FOLLOW UP

Exercise 5

Work with a partner.

One student is the tenant and looks at page 67. The other student is the landlord and looks at this page.

The tenant draws the problems in the apartment and then tells the landlord about them. The landlord draws each problem.

Look at each other's page and make sure they are the same.

Then change roles.

TENANT: We've got problems.
LANDLORD: What's the matter?
TENANT: The lock's broken, the radiator leaks, and . . .
LANDLORD: I'll take care of it tomorrow.

TAPESCRIPT

UNIT 1

What do we need?

Look at the pictures and listen.

1. HUSBAND: What do we need, honey?
   WIFE: Let's see. We need some flour. We don't have any.

2. HUSBAND: Eggs?
   WIFE: Eggs? Uh, yeah. We're all out.

3. HUSBAND: Milk?
   WIFE: Uh-huh.

4. HUSBAND: Cooking oil?
   WIFE: What?
   HUSBAND: Do we need oil?
   WIFE: Yes. We need some. We're almost out. Watch the eggs!

5. WIFE: Um, cereal. Do we need cereal?
   HUSBAND: Uh, I think we have some, but let's get another box. How about corn flakes?
   WIFE: OK.

6. WIFE: And we need a loaf of bread.
   HUSBAND: How about some Italian bread?
   WIFE: That's fine.

7. WIFE: Hm. Cookies. Let's ask. Excuse me, where are the cookies?
   STOCKPERSON: They're in aisle 5, ma'am.
   WIFE: Aisle 5. OK. Thanks. Here they are.
   HUSBAND: What else, dear?

8. WIFE: Laundry detergent. Excuse me, where is the laundry detergent?
   STOCKPERSON: It's in aisle 4.
   WIFE: Thank you.
   HUSBAND: OK. Here it is. Let's go.

9. WIFE: Oh! The eggs! Look what you've done!

Now look at the pictures again and listen.

(*Repetition of above*)

Exercise 1

Listen to the conversations. Match the conversations with the pictures.

1. HUSBAND: Cooking oil!
   WIFE: What?
   HUSBAND: Do we need cooking oil?
   WIFE: Yes.

2. HUSBAND: Flour?
   WIFE: Yes. We're all out.

3. WIFE: Where are the eggs?
   STOCKPERSON: They're in aisle 1.
   WIFE: Thanks.

4. WIFE: Bread?
   HUSBAND: Oh! Yes. We don't have any.

5. HUSBAND: Excuse me, where is the laundry detergent?
   STOCKPERSON: It's in aisle 3, sir.

6. WIFE: Oh! Cookies!
   HUSBAND: Yeah. We need some.

7. HUSBAND: Do we need milk?
   WIFE: Uh-huh. We're almost out.

8. HUSBAND: How about cereal?
   WIFE: Uh, we don't have any. Let's get corn flakes.

Exercise 2

Number the sentences as you hear them.

HUSBAND: Do we need flour?
WIFE: Yes, we're almost out.
HUSBAND: Laundry detergent?
WIFE: Yeah, we don't have any. Oh! We need milk and eggs.
HUSBAND: Excuse me, where is the cooking oil?
STOCKPERSON: It's in aisle 3.
HUSBAND: And the cookies?
STOCKPERSON: They're in aisle 4.
HUSBAND: Anything else?
WIFE: Yes, we need a loaf of bread and some cereal.

Exercise 3

Listen and circle the words you hear.

1. We need milk and eggs.
2. Excuse me, where's the cooking oil?
3. We don't have any bread or cereal.
4. What do we need? Uh, let's see. Flour, laundry detergent, and milk.
5. We need bread and uh, we're all out of flour and oil.
6. Excuse me. Where are the cookies and the eggs?

Exercise 4

Look at the pictures and listen.

SHOPPER: Excuse me. Where're the noodles?
STOCKPERSON: They're in aisle 4, ma'am.
SHOPPER: And the rice?
STOCKPERSON: In aisle 5.

SHOPPER: Where's the toilet paper?
STOCKPERSON: It's in aisle 1.
SHOPPER: And where're the hot dogs?
STOCKPERSON: In aisle 6.
SHOPPER: Thank you.

SHOPPER: Where's the tea?
STOCKPERSON: In aisle 3.
SHOPPER: And the peanuts?
STOCKPERSON: They're also in aisle 3.
SHOPPER: Thanks.

Now listen again and write the aisle number.

(*Repetition of above*)

Exercise 5

Listen and circle the verb you hear.

1. Excuse me, where're the peanuts?
2. The toilet paper's in aisle 3.
3. Where's the cereal?
4. Excuse me, where're the eggs?
5. Hot dogs are in aisle 1.
6. Bread's in aisle 2.

Exercise 6

Listen and check the items you hear in each conversation.

1. MOTHER: What do we need?
   DAUGHTER: Noodles. Oh, and flour. We're all out.
   MOTHER: OK.

2. SHOPPER: Excuse me, where are the hot dogs?
   STOCKPERSON: They're in aisle 6, sir.
   SHOPPER: And the peanuts?
   STOCKPERSON: Aisle 2.
   SHOPPER: Thank you.

3. SHOPPER: Excuse me, where's the cooking oil?
   STOCKPERSON: Oil? Oh, it's in aisle 3.
   SHOPPER: And the noodles?
   STOCKPERSON: They're also in aisle 3.
   SHOPPER: Thanks.

4. WIFE: We need a loaf of bread.
   HUSBAND: How about Italian?
   WIFE: OK.
   HUSBAND: What else? Cookies?
   WIFE: Uh-huh.
   HUSBAND: How about these?
   WIFE: Fine. Now, let's see. Where are the noodles and the rice?
   HUSBAND: Noodles and rice? In the next aisle, I think.

5. DAUGHTER: Dad, we need some eggs.
   FATHER: Uh-huh. Milk, too. We're all out.
   DAUGHTER: Do we need toilet paper?
   FATHER: Yes, I think so.
   DAUGHTER: Where are the hot dogs?
   FATHER: Over here. OK, what else?
   DAUGHTER: We need cookies and cereal. And can we get peanuts?
   FATHER: Sure.

UNIT 2

How much is this first class?

Look at the pictures and listen.

1. CUSTOMER: How much is this first class?
   CLERK: First class? Let's see. You need sixty-five cents on it. And don't forget the zip code.
   CUSTOMER: Oh, sorry. Let's see. It's, uh, 0-2-1-3-9.

2. CUSTOMER: And this letter is airmail.
   CLERK: OK. Airmail to Venezuela is forty-five cents.

3. CUSTOMER: I'd also like six 25-cent stamps.

4. CUSTOMER: Three 45-cent stamps.
   CLERK: Uh-huh.

5. CUSTOMER: And one 15-cent stamp.

6. CLERK: Anything else?
   CUSTOMER: Uh, yes. One aerogramme, please.
   CLERK: Here you are.

7. CLERK: Let me add that up. Sixty-five, forty-five, a dollar fifty, one thirty-five, fifteen, and thirty-nine—altogether that's four dollars and forty-nine cents.

Now look at the pictures again and listen.

(*Repetition of above*)

Exercise 1

Listen and circle the item you hear.

1. CUSTOMER: Hi, I'd like three aerogrammes, please.
   CLERK: Here you are.

2. CLERK: Anything else?
   CUSTOMER: Yes. Four 15-cent stamps.
   CLERK: OK.

3. CUSTOMER: And how much is this letter first class?
   CLERK: Let's see. You need sixty-five cents on it.
   CUSTOMER: OK.

4. CLERK: What's the zip code?
   CUSTOMER: Oops! Let's see. It's 2-0-9-0-2.

5. CUSTOMER: I also need a 25-cent stamp.

6. CLERK: OK. Is that it?
   CUSTOMER: Yes.
   CLERK: Altogether that's two sixty-seven.

Exercise 2

Number the sentences as you hear them.

CUSTOMER: How much is this first class?
CLERK: First class? Let's see. You need sixty-five cents on it. And don't forget the zip code.
CUSTOMER: Oh, sorry. It's 02139. And this letter is airmail.
CLERK: OK. Air mail to Venezuela is forty-five cents.
CUSTOMER: I'd also like six 25-cent stamps and one 15-cent stamp.
CLERK: Anything else?
CUSTOMER: Yes. One aerogramme, please.
CLERK: Here you are. Altogether that's four dollars and forty-nine cents.

Exercise 3

Can you predict what the clerk will say? Listen and circle the response.

1. How much is this letter first class?
2. I need two aerogrammes.

3. This letter is airmail.
4. I'd like three 25-cent stamps.
5. Let's see. I need two 45-cent stamps.

Exercise 4

Look at the pictures and listen.

1. CUSTOMER: How much is this package third class?
   CLERK: Third class?
   CUSTOMER: Yes.
   CLERK: Uh, that's three dollars.

2. CLERK: Next!
   CUSTOMER: Hi. I'd like a book of twenty-five-cent stamps.
   CLERK: OK. Here you are. Anything else?
   CUSTOMER: No, thanks.
   CLERK: That's five dollars.

3. CLERK: Next please!
   CUSTOMER: I'd like a money order, please.
   CLERK: For what amount?
   CUSTOMER: Ten dollars.
   CLERK: All right. There's a seventy-five-cent charge. So, that's ten seventy-five, altogether.

4. CLERK: Next.
   CUSTOMER: Hi. I'd like, um, five postcards.
   CLERK: OK. They're fifteen cents each. Altogether, that's seventy-five cents.

Now listen again and write the price.

(Repetition of above)

Exercise 5

Listen and check the items you hear in each conversation. Write how many of each item the customer wants.

1. CUSTOMER: Hello. I'd like three 15-cent stamps, please. Uh, and two 20-cent stamps.
   CLERK: How many 20-cent?
   CUSTOMER: Two. And two books of stamps.
   CLERK: Here you go. Anything else?
   CUSTOMER: Yes. I need a money order for ten dollars.

2. CLERK: Next!
   CUSTOMER: Hi. I need five aerogrammes, please. And, um, some stamps. Let's see. Ten 25-cent stamps and twenty 15-cent stamps.
   CLERK: Is that it?
   CUSTOMER: Uh, give me five postcards, too.
   CLERK: OK. Here you go.

3. CLERK: Next, please!
   CUSTOMER: I'd like two money orders, please.
   CLERK: For what amounts?
   CUSTOMER: Ten dollars each.
   CLERK: Anything else?
   CUSTOMER: Yes. Fifteen 45-cent stamps, and, uh, two postcards.

4. CLERK: Next!
   CUSTOMER: Hi. I'd like three books of stamps, please. And, um, ten 15-cent stamps.

CLERK: 15-cent stamps?
CUSTOMER: Uh-huh. Ten. And, um, two 20- cent stamps.
CLERK: Anything else?
CUSTOMER: Yes, an aerogramme.

UNIT 3

Four pounds of apples, please.

Look at the pictures and listen.

1. SHOPPER: Four pounds of apples, please.
   FARMER: OK.

2. FARMER: Anything else?
   SHOPPER: Yes. Two pounds of potatoes.
   FARMER: Uh-huh.

3. SHOPPER: A head of lettuce.

4. SHOPPER: And, uh, some radishes.
   FARMER: One bunch?
   SHOPPER: Yes.
   FARMER: Is that all?
   SHOPPER: That's it.
   FARMER: Four dollars. Thank you. Have a good day!
   SHOPPER: You too.

5. FARMER: May I help you?
   SHOPPER: Yes, I'd like a pound and a half of onions.
   FARMER: OK.

6. FARMER: What else?
   SHOPPER: Hm. Some cheese. How much is it?
   FARMER: Four dollars a pound.

7. SHOPPER: All right. Give me a quarter of a pound.
   FARMER: Anything else?
   SHOPPER: No, that's all.

Now look at the pictures again and listen.

(Repetition of above)

Exercise 1

Listen and circle the items you hear.

FARMER: May I help you?
SHOPPER: Yes, I'd like a half a pound of cheese, please.
FARMER: OK. Anything else?
SHOPPER: Yes, how much are the onions?
FARMER: Forty-five cents a pound.
SHOPPER: OK. Give me two pounds.
FARMER: What else?
SHOPPER: Five pounds of apples. And, uh, a bunch of radishes.
FARMER: Is that all?
SHOPPER: Yes, that's it.

Exercise 2

Listen and circle the items you hear.

SHOPPER: I'd like three pounds of potatoes, please.
FARMER: All right. What else?
SHOPPER: How much is the cheese?
FARMER: Five fifty a pound.

SHOPPER: OK. Give me a pound, please.
FARMER: Is that it?
SHOPPER: No. I want a head of lettuce and a pound of onions.
FARMER: OK.

Exercise 3

Number the sentences as you hear them.

FARMER: May I help you?
SHOPPER: Yes, I'd like a pound and a half of onions.
FARMER: OK. What else?
SHOPPER: Hm, some cheese. How much is it?
FARMER: Four dollars a pound.
SHOPPER: All right. Give me a quarter of a pound.
FARMER: Anything else?
SHOPPER: No, that's all.

Exercise 4

Complete the conversation.

FARMER: May I help you?
SHOPPER: Yes, I'd like a head of lettuce and a bunch of radishes.
FARMER: OK.
SHOPPER: I need three pounds of potatoes too.
FARMER: What else?
SHOPPER: Two pounds of apples.
FARMER: Anything else?
SHOPPER: How much is the cheese?
FARMER: Four twenty-five a pound.
SHOPPER: OK. Give me half a pound.

Exercise 5

Look at the pictures and listen.

WIFE: Hi, honey. What did you buy?
HUSBAND: A pound of bananas. Two pounds of tomatoes. A box of strawberries.
WIFE: Mmm. What else?
HUSBAND: A dozen eggs. A bunch of carrots. And a half a pound of green beans.
WIFE: Good. Let's have lunch.

Now listen again and match the words with the pictures.

(*Repetition of above*)

Exercise 6

Listen and write how much of each item the customer wants.

1. CUSTOMER: Hi. How much is this cheese?
   FARMER: Four fifty a pound.
   CUSTOMER: OK. Give me a quarter of a pound, please.
   FARMER: What else?
   CUSTOMER: A box of strawberries, please.
2. CUSTOMER: Five pounds of onions, please. How much are the bananas?
   FARMER: Thirty-nine cents a pound.
   CUSTOMER: OK. Give me three pounds, please.
   FARMER: Anything else?

CUSTOMER: Yes. I'd like a box of strawberries. And that's it.
FARMER: OK.

3. FARMER: May I help you?
   CUSTOMER: Two pounds of apples, please. And three bunches of carrots.
   FARMER: Anything else?
   CUSTOMER: Um, yes. Give me a half a pound of green beans.
   FARMER: Is that it?
   CUSTOMER: Yes, thanks.
4. FARMER: Yes?
   CUSTOMER: Two pounds of tomatoes, please. And a head of lettuce.
   FARMER: What else?
   CUSTOMER: Uh, a half a pound of cheese.
   FARMER: OK. Is that it?
   CUSTOMER: Uh, two bunches of radishes.
5. FARMER: May I help you?
   CUSTOMER: Yes, I'd like three pounds of potatoes, please.
   FARMER: OK. Anything else?
   CUSTOMER: Yes, two dozen eggs. And, uh, some strawberries. Three boxes.
   FARMER: Is that it?
   CUSTOMER: No. I'd like a bunch of carrots too.
   FARMER: OK.

UNIT 4

Do you have white semi-gloss paint?

Look at the pictures and listen.

1. CUSTOMER: Do you have white semi-gloss paint?
   CLERK: Yes, we do. What size do you need? Gallon or quart?
   CUSTOMER: Gallon.
2. CLERK: Do you need a paintbrush?
   CUSTOMER: Paintbrush? Yes, actually, I do.
   CLERK: We have many sizes. Wide or narrow?
   CUSTOMER: Narrow.
   CLERK: All right. How's this?
   CUSTOMER: Fine.
   CLERK: Is that it?
3. CUSTOMER: Let's see. Oh, I need a few hooks.
   CLERK: Over here. We have all sizes. Do you need large or small?
   CUSTOMER: Large. I'll take two.
4. CUSTOMER: Oh, excuse me. I need some batteries, too.
   CLERK: What kind?
   CUSTOMER: For my Walkman.
   CLERK: OK. These are four for $2.49.
   CUSTOMER: Fine.

Now look at the pictures again and listen.

(*Repetition of above*)

Exercise 1

Listen and circle each item the customer wants.

1. CUSTOMER: I need a paintbrush.
   CLERK: What kind?
   CUSTOMER: I think a wide one.
   CLERK: How about this size?
   CUSTOMER: That's good.

2. CUSTOMER: I need some white semi-gloss paint.
   CLERK: Quart or gallon?
   CUSTOMER: Quart.

3. CLERK: Do you need a paintbrush?
   CUSTOMER: Yes, I do. A wide one. Oh! And I need some batteries.

4. CLERK: May I help you?
   CUSTOMER: Yes, I need a very narrow paintbrush. Oh, and where are the hooks?
   CLERK: They're over here. What size do you need? Large or small?
   CUSTOMER: Large.

5. CUSTOMER: Do you have white semi-gloss paint?
   CLERK: Yes, we do.
   CUSTOMER: I need a gallon.
   CLERK: Anything else?
   CUSTOMER: Do you have hooks?
   CLERK: Uh-huh. Over here. What kind?
   CUSTOMER: Some small ones.

6. CLERK: May I help you?
   CUSTOMER: Yes, I need a small hook and some batteries for my radio.
   CLERK: OK. Anything else?
   CUSTOMER: No, that's it.

7. CUSTOMER: Do you have batteries?
   CLERK: Yes, we do. Here they are.
   CUSTOMER: OK. These are fine. I also need a paintbrush.
   CLERK: What size?
   CUSTOMER: A wide one.

Exercise 2

Number the sentences as you hear them.

CUSTOMER: I need a gallon of white semi-gloss paint.
CLERK: Here it is. Do you need a paintbrush?
CUSTOMER: Yes, actually, I do.
CLERK: We have many sizes. Wide or narrow?
CUSTOMER: Narrow.
CLERK: All right. How's this?
CUSTOMER: Fine. Oh, and I need a few hooks.
CLERK: Over here. We have all sizes. Large? Small?
CUSTOMER: Large. I'll take two. Oh, excuse me. I need some batteries, too.

Exercise 3

Listen and check the words you hear.

1. I need a gallon of paint and a small paintbrush.
2. Hooks? We have many sizes.
3. I'll take two paintbrushes and some batteries.
4. Do you have a quart of white semi-gloss paint?
5. Do you need batteries, too?

6. I need a few large hooks.

Exercise 4

Look at the pictures and listen.

1. CUSTOMER: Do you have masking tape?
   CLERK: Masking tape? Yes, over here.
   CUSTOMER: I need some screws, too. And a screwdriver.

2. CLERK: May I help you?
   CUSTOMER: Yes, do you have extension cords?
   CLERK: Uh-huh. What size? A short or long one? We have 6 feet, 10 feet and 12 feet.
   CUSTOMER: Um, 12 feet is fine.
   CLERK: What else?
   CUSTOMER: Mm. I need a hammer and some nails.

3. CUSTOMER: Where are the lightbulbs?
   CLERK: Lightbulbs? Over here.
   CUSTOMER: Uh, I need a 100-watt bulb and a 60-watt bulb.
   CLERK: A hundred and a sixty. OK. Anything else?
   CUSTOMER: And a pair of scissors.
   CLERK: Scissors are over here.

Now listen again and number the words as you hear them.

(Repetition of above)

Exercise 5

Listen and check the items each customer wants. Circle the size of the items.

1. CLERK: May I help you?
   CUSTOMER: Yes, I need an extension cord.
   CLERK: How long?
   CUSTOMER: Mm, let's see. Ten feet.
   CLERK: OK. Anything else?
   CUSTOMER: Yeah, I need some masking tape.
   CLERK: Wide? Narrow?
   CUSTOMER: Uh, wide. Oh, and some screws.

2. CUSTOMER: Excuse me, do you have white semi-gloss paint?
   CLERK: Yes.
   CUSTOMER: I need a quart.
   CLERK: OK. Do you need a brush?
   CUSTOMER: No, but I need a lightbulb. A hundred watts.
   CLERK: What else?
   CUSTOMER: Do you have hooks?
   CLERK: Large or small?
   CUSTOMER: Uh, small.
   CLERK: Over here.
   CUSTOMER: I'll take two.

3. CLERK: May I help you?
   CUSTOMER: Yes, I need some white paint. A gallon is enough, I think. Oh, and a paintbrush.
   CLERK: We have many different sizes.
   CUSTOMER: I need a wide one.
   CLERK: OK. Is that it?
   CUSTOMER: Where are the scissors?

CLERK: Over here.
CUSTOMER: I need a small pair.
CLERK: OK.
CUSTOMER: And lightbulbs. I need a sixty and a hundred watt bulb.

4. CUSTOMER: Excuse me, where are the nails?
CLERK: This way.
CUSTOMER: Yes, these are fine. I also need a hammer.
CLERK: Anything else?
CUSTOMER: Masking tape.
CLERK: What size?
CUSTOMER: Narrow. And I need some batteries for my radio.
CLERK: These are two for $2.20.
CUSTOMER: Fine.

UNIT 5
Do you want a ride home?

Look at the pictures and listen.

WOMAN: Do you want a ride home, Paul?
MAN: Yeah, sure. Thanks.
WOMAN: Now, how do I get to your place?
1. MAN: Uh, go straight to the light.
2. MAN: Then turn left.
WOMAN: At the light?
MAN: Yeah, left.
3. WOMAN: Straight?
MAN: Uh-huh. Go over the bridge.
4. MAN: Make a right.
WOMAN: OK.
5. MAN: Turn right at the first intersection.
WOMAN: First intersection?
MAN: Right.
6. MAN: OK. It's the second house on the left.
WOMAN: Second on the left. Here?
MAN: Yep! Thanks a million, Julie. See you tomorrow. Bye!
WOMAN: Bye!

Now look at the pictures again and listen.

(*Repetition of above*)

Exercise 1

Listen and circle the picture that matches what you hear.

1. A: Now how do I get to your place?
   B: Make a right at the light.
2. A: Which house?
   B: It's the first house on the right.
3. A: Straight?
   B: Yes, go straight over the bridge.
4. A: Which house?
   B: It's the second house on the left.
5. A: How do I get to your place?
   B: Go straight to the light.

6. A: Straight?
   B: No, turn left at the intersection.
7. A: Which house?
   B: It's the first house on the left.

Exercise 2

Number the sentences as you hear them.

WOMAN: Do you want a ride home, Paul?
MAN: Yeah, sure. Thanks.
WOMAN: Now, how do I get to your place?
MAN: Go straight to the light. Then turn left.
WOMAN: At the light?
MAN: Yeah. Left.
WOMAN: Straight?
MAN: Uh-huh. Go over the bridge and turn right at the first intersection.
WOMAN: OK.
MAN: It's the second house on the left.

Exercise 3

Listen and circle the words you hear.

1. Go straight to the light.
2. Make a left at the first intersection.
3. It's the first house over the bridge.
4. It's the second house on the right.
5. Turn right at the second light.

Exercise 4

Look at the map and listen.

1. **Begin at START and find the art museum.**
   A: Excuse me. How do I get to the art museum?
   B: Go straight four blocks.
   A: OK. Straight four blocks . . .
   B: Then turn right. It's the third building on the left.
   A: Third building on the left. OK. Thank you.

2. **Go back to START and find the bank.**
   A: Pardon me. Where's the bank?
   B: The bank? Uh, go straight three blocks and turn right.
   A: OK.
   B: Uh, it's the second building on the left.
   A: Second on the left. Thanks a lot.

3. **Go back to START and find the bus station.**
   A: How do I get to the bus station?
   B: Go straight one block. Turn left. It's, uh, the fifth building on the right.
   A: Fifth building on the right. Thank you!

4. **Go back to START and find the library.**
   A: Excuse me. Where's the library?
   B: Go two blocks and turn right.
   A: OK.
   B: It's the fourth building on the left.
   A: Fourth building? OK. Thanks very much.

5. Go back to START and find the post office.

A: Pardon me. How do I get to the post office?
B: Go straight four blocks and turn right. It's the first building on the left.
A: All right. Thanks a lot.

Now listen again and write the names on the map.

(*Repetition of above*)

Exercise 5

Listen to the conversations. Find the house or apartment building and circle it.

1. Begin at START.

A: Where's your house?
B: Uh, go straight to the second light.
A: OK.
B: Then make a left.
A: Uh-huh . . .
B: At the second intersection, turn right, and it's the first house on the left.
A: First house on the left. OK. See you later. Bye!

2. Begin at START.

A: How do I get to your place?
B: Turn right at the first intersection. OK?
A: OK.
B: Then go straight two blocks, and go over a bridge.
A: A bridge? OK.
B: Then turn left. At the first light, make a right.
A: A right at the light.
B: Yes. It's the third building on the right.
A: Third on the right. OK. Thanks. See you later!

3. Begin at START.

A: How do I get to your apartment?
B: Go straight from here and turn right at the third intersection.
A: Uh-huh. Third intersection.
B: Then go straight to the light and make a left.
A: A left at the light?
B: Yes. My apartment is in the fifth building on the right.
A: Fifth on the right. OK. Thanks.
B: See you tomorrow! Bye.

4. Begin at START.

A: How do I get to your house from here?
B: Go straight to the first light and make a left.
A: Left at the light. OK.
B: Then go one block and turn right.
A: OK.
B: It's the fourth house on the right.
A: Fourth house. All right. Thanks. See you later.

UNIT 6

What time is the next train to White Plains?

Look at the pictures and listen.

1. TRAVELER: What time is the next train to White Plains?

INFORMATION: White Plains? There's one at 2:30.
TRAVELER: Is it local or express?
INFORMATION: Local.

2. TRAVELER: OK. When does it arrive?
INFORMATION: 3:22.
TRAVELER: 3:22?
INFORMATION: That's right.

3. TRAVELER: And where do I buy a ticket?
INFORMATION: Over there. Window 11.
TRAVELER: Thanks.

4. TRAVELER: A ticket to White Plains, please.
CLERK: One way?
TRAVELER: Uh, no, round trip.

5. CLERK: That's $7.50.
TRAVELER: OK. Here you are.

6. TRAVELER: I need a receipt, please.
CLERK: OK.

7. TRAVELER: Where do I catch the train?
CLERK: It leaves from Track 25.
TRAVELER: Track 25. OK. Thanks.

Now look at the pictures again and listen.

(*Repetition of above*)

Exercise 1

Listen to the conversations. Circle the pictures that match what you hear.

1. TRAVELER: Pardon me, what time is the next train to Los Angeles?
INFORMATION: There's one at 3:00.
TRAVELER: Where do I catch it?
INFORMATION: Track 1.
TRAVELER: Thanks a lot.

2. TRAVELER: A one-way ticket to Boston, please.
CLERK: OK. That's ten dollars.
TRAVELER: Here you are.
CLERK: The train leaves in ten minutes from Track 12.
TRAVELER: 12?
CLERK: Yes.
TRAVELER: Thanks.

3. TRAVELER: What time is the next train to Princeton?
CLERK: At 2:00.
TRAVELER: I'd like a round-trip ticket, please. And a receipt.
CLERK: OK. That's $7.50.

4. TRAVELER: Excuse me. Where do I get the train to Chicago?
CLERK: It leaves from Track 8 in ten minutes.
TRAVELER: Ten minutes? OK. I'd like a one-way ticket, please.

5. TRAVELER: Excuse me, where do I buy a ticket to New York?
INFORMATION: Window 5.
TRAVELER: Thanks. I'd like a ticket to New York, please.
CLERK: One way?
TRAVELER: Uh-huh.
CLERK: Here you are. That's ten dollars.

6. TRAVELER: Pardon me, when is the next train to Washington?
INFORMATION: There's one at 9:45.
TRAVELER: What time does it arrive?
INFORMATION: At 12:00. It's express.
TRAVELER: Where do I buy a ticket?
INFORMATION: Go to window 1.
TRAVELER: Thank you.

Exercise 2

Number the sentences as you hear them.

TRAVELER: What time is the next train to White Plains?
INFORMATION: There's one at 2:30.
TRAVELER: Is it local or express?
INFORMATION: Local.
TRAVELER: When does it arrive?
INFORMATION: 3:22.
TRAVELER: Where do I buy a ticket?
INFORMATION: Window 11.
TRAVELER: A round-trip ticket to White Plains, please.
CLERK: OK. Here you are. It leaves from Track 25.

Exercise 3

Can you predict what the clerk will say? Listen and circle the response.

1. Excuse me. Where do I buy a ticket?
2. A one-way ticket to New York, please.
3. Is it local or express?
4. When does the train arrive?
5. Where do I catch the train?
6. Can you give me a receipt, please?

Exercise 4

Look at the schedule and listen to a part of each conversation.

1. INFORMATION: Train information.
TRAVELER: Yes, hello. What's your daily schedule to Boston?
INFORMATION: The first train is at 6:00 A.M. arriving at 10:00 A.M. There's one at 9:13 A.M. arriving at 12:30 P.M. It's express.

2. INFORMATION: Midwest Air. May I help you?
TRAVELER: Yes. What's your daily flight schedule from Chicago to Detroit?
INFORMATION: Uh, let's see. Our first flight is at 5:18 A.M. arriving at 6:10 A.M. There's one at 8:00 A.M. arriving at 8:50 A.M.

3. INFORMATION: Bus information.
TRAVELER: What's your daily schedule to Philadelphia, please?
INFORMATION: There's a bus at 6:45 A.M. arriving at 8:30 in the morning. One at 10:04 A.M. arriving at 12:15 P.M.

TRAVELER: 10:04 arriving 12:15?
INFORMATION: That's right.

Now listen again and complete the schedules.

1. INFORMATION: Train information.
TRAVELER: Yes, hello. What's your daily schedule to Boston?
INFORMATION: The first train's at 6:00 A.M. arriving at 10:00 A.M. There's one at 9:13 A.M. arriving at 12:30 P.M. It's express.
TRAVELER: OK.
INFORMATION: Uh, one at 1:20 P.M. arriving at 5:05 P.M.
TRAVELER: It leaves at 1:20?
INFORMATION: Yes. Arriving at 5:05. And one at 4:55 P.M. arriving at 9:02 P.M.
TRAVELER: OK. Thanks very much.

2. INFORMATION: Midwest Air. May I help you?
TRAVELER: Yes. What's your daily flight schedule from Chicago to Detroit?
INFORMATION: Uh, let's see. Our first flight is at 5:18 A.M. arriving at 6:10 A.M. There's one at 8:00 A.M. arriving at 8:50 A.M.
TRAVELER: Um, OK. Is there anything later?
INFORMATION: Yes, there's one at 1:40 P.M. arriving at 2:30 P.M.
TRAVELER: Uh-huh.
INFORMATION: The last one leaves at 6:15 arriving at 7:05 P.M.
TRAVELER: 6:15 P.M. arriving at 7:05. OK. Thanks a lot.

3. INFORMATION: Bus information.
TRAVELER: What's your daily schedule to Philadelphia, please?
INFORMATION: There's a bus at 6:45 A.M. arriving at 8:30 A.M. and one at 10:04 A.M. arriving at 12:15 P.M.
TRAVELER: 10:04 arriving 12:15?
INFORMATION: That's right. There's also one at 3:08 P.M. arriving at 5:35 P.M. And one at 7:50 P.M. arriving at 10:10.
TRAVELER: 7:50 arriving at 10:10 at night. Thank you.

Exercise 5

Listen and write the information you hear.

1. TRAVELER: What time is the next train to Pittsburgh?
INFORMATION: Uh, there's one at 2:30.
TRAVELER: And where do I buy a ticket?
INFORMATION: Window 5.
TRAVELER: Thank you.
TRAVELER: I'd like a round-trip ticket to Pittsburgh, please.
CLERK: OK. That's seven fifty.
TRAVELER: Here you are. Where do I catch the train?
CLERK: Track 15.
TRAVELER: Thanks!

2. TRAVELER: I'd like a ticket to Rochester, please.
CLERK: Round trip?
TRAVELER: No, one way.

CLERK:	That's nine twenty-five.	
TRAVELER:	What time does it leave?	
CLERK:	Um, five o'clock, track 8.	
TRAVELER:	Which track?	
CLERK:	8.	
TRAVELER:	OK. Thanks.	

3.
TRAVELER:	What time is the next train for Denver?
INFORMATION:	There's one at 6:45.
TRAVELER:	What time does it arrive?
INFORMATION:	Ah, let's see. 10:15.
TRAVELER:	And where do I buy a ticket?
INFORMATION:	Window 7.

4.
TRAVELER:	Round trip to Boston, please.
CLERK:	That's twelve ninety-five.
TRAVELER:	Here you are.
CLERK:	The train leaves from track 14.
TRAVELER:	At what time?
CLERK:	There's one at 6:13.
TRAVELER:	OK. Thanks.

5.
TRAVELER:	When's the next train to Washington?
INFORMATION:	There's one at 9:00.
TRAVELER:	What time does it arrive?
INFORMATION:	10:44.
TRAVELER:	Where can I catch it?
INFORMATION:	Over there. Track 4.
TRAVELER:	Thanks a lot.

UNIT 7
Can I see the sweater in the window?

Look at the pictures and listen.

1.
CUSTOMER:	Can I see the sweater in the window?
CLERK:	Sure. The white one?
CUSTOMER:	Uh-huh.

2.
CLERK:	Here they are. What size do you need?
CUSTOMER:	Um . . .
CLERK:	They run small, medium, and large.
CUSTOMER:	Oh. Uh, probably a medium.

3.
CUSTOMER:	How much is it?
CLERK:	It's on sale for twelve dollars.

4.
CUSTOMER:	I'm also looking for a black cotton skirt, size 10.
CLERK:	How about this?
CUSTOMER:	No, I don't really like the style. It's too long.

5.
CLERK:	We have this one in black, too.
CUSTOMER:	Oh, that's nice.

6.
CUSTOMER:	Where can I try it on?
CLERK:	The dressing rooms are over here.

Now look at the pictures again and listen.

(Repetition of above)

Exercise 1

Listen to the conversations. Circle the picture that matches what you hear.

1.
CUSTOMER:	Hi, can I see the black sweater in the window?
CLERK:	Sure. They're over here.

2.
CLERK:	What's your size?
CUSTOMER:	Mm, probably a small.

3.
CUSTOMER:	Is it on sale?
CLERK:	No, it's not.

4.
CUSTOMER:	Where can I try it on?
CLERK:	The dressing rooms are over here.

5.
CUSTOMER:	Oh, I'm also looking for a short skirt.
CLERK:	OK. They're over here.

6.
CLERK:	What size?
CUSTOMER:	How do they run?
CLERK:	Small, medium, and large.
CUSTOMER:	Uh, medium.
CLERK:	This one's on sale.
CUSTOMER:	Oh, that's nice. How much is it?
CLERK:	It's on sale for $24.99.

Exercise 2

Number the sentences as you hear them.

CUSTOMER:	Can I see that sweater? The white one in the window?
CLERK:	Sure. What size do you need? They run small, medium, and large.
CUSTOMER:	Oh, probably a medium. How much is it?
CLERK:	It's on sale for twelve dollars.
CUSTOMER:	I'm also looking for a black cotton skirt, size 10.
CLERK:	How about this?
CUSTOMER:	Oh, that's nice. Where can I try it on?
CLERK:	The dressing rooms are over there.

Exercise 3

Can you predict what the clerk will say? Listen and circle the response.

1. Can I see the skirt in the window?
2. How much is it?
3. What sizes do you have?
4. Where can I try it on?
5. I'm looking for a black sweater.
6. Is it on sale?

Exercise 4

Look at the pictures and listen.

1.
CUSTOMER:	Can I see the jacket in the window?
CLERK:	Sure. The blue one?
CUSTOMER:	Yes.
CLERK:	What size do you need?

2.
CUSTOMER:	Excuse me. I'm looking for a blouse.
CLERK:	Blouses are over here. What size do you wear?
CUSTOMER:	Small.
CLERK:	How about this?

3.
CLERK:	May I help you?
CUSTOMER:	Yes, where can I try on these pants?

4. CUSTOMER: Excuse me, can I please see that shirt in the window?
   CLERK: Sure. The striped one?
   CUSTOMER: Uh-huh. How much is it?
5. CUSTOMER: I'm looking for some leather gloves.
   CLERK: Gloves are over here. How about these?

Can you predict what the people will say? Listen again and circle the response.

(*Repetition of above*)

Exercise 5

Listen and number the pictures as you hear them.

1. CUSTOMER: How much is this shirt?
   CLERK: It's fifteen dollars.
   CUSTOMER: I'm also looking for a black skirt.
   CLERK: Sure. Skirts are over here.
2. CUSTOMER: Excuse me, is the jacket in the window on sale?
   CLERK: Yes, it's now twenty dollars.
   CUSTOMER: Can I see it?
   CLERK: Sure. What's your size? They run small, medium, and large.
   CUSTOMER: Probably large.
3. CLERK: May I help you?
   CUSTOMER: Yes, I'd like this sweater. And I'm looking for some leather gloves.
   CLERK: We have these.
   CUSTOMER: How much are they?
   CLERK: Thirty dollars.
   CUSTOMER: Oh, that's too expensive.
4. CUSTOMER: I'm looking for a cotton blouse.
   CLERK: Sure. What size do you wear?
   CUSTOMER: Medium, I think. And can I see that shirt, too? The striped one?
   CLERK: OK.
5. CUSTOMER: Excuse me, where are the dressing rooms? I'd like to try on these pants?
   CLERK: Sure. They're over here. Are you looking for a shirt, too?
   CUSTOMER: I don't think so. Thanks.

UNIT 8

Are you busy right now?

Look at the pictures and listen.

MAN: Excuse me, Sara, are you busy right now?
WOMAN: Not really. What do you need?
MAN: Can you show me how to use this machine?
WOMAN: Sure.
1. WOMAN: Turn it on here.
   MAN: Uh-huh.
2. WOMAN: Insert the paper tray like this. OK?
   MAN: Yes, OK.
3. WOMAN: Then put your paper here, face down.
4. WOMAN: How many copies do you want?
   MAN: Uh, seven.
   WOMAN: OK. Press 7.

MAN: Oh, I see. OK.
5. WOMAN: Now, press the start button. Here.
6. WOMAN: Now, turn off the machine.
   MAN: OK. I got it. Thanks a lot, Sara.
   WOMAN: Anytime.

Now look at the pictures again and listen.

(*Repetition of above*)

Exercise 1

Listen to the conversations. Match the conversations with the pictures.

1. WOMAN: Press the start button.
   MAN: This?
   WOMAN: Uh-huh. That's right.
2. MAN: Can you show me how to insert the paper tray?
   WOMAN: Sure. Like this.
   MAN: Oh, I see. Thanks.
3. WOMAN: Put the paper here, face down.
4. MAN: Can you show me how to turn off this machine?
   WOMAN: Sure. Like this.
5. WOMAN: How many copies do you want?
   MAN: Seventy.
   WOMAN: OK. Press seven-zero.
   MAN: Thanks.
6. WOMAN: Do you need help with that machine?
   MAN: Yeah.
   WOMAN: Turn it on here.

Exercise 2

Number the sentences as you hear them.

MAN: Excuse me, Sara. Can you show me how to use this machine?
WOMAN: Sure.
Turn it on here.
Insert the paper tray like this.
Then put your paper here, face down.
How many copies do you want?
MAN: Seven.
WOMAN: OK. Press 7.
Now press the start button.
Then turn off the machine.

Exercise 3

Complete the conversations.

WOMAN: Excuse me. Are you busy right now?
MAN: Not really. What do you need?
WOMAN: How do you use this machine? I need ten copies.
MAN: OK. Turn it on here. Then insert the paper tray, like this. Put your paper here. Press 10. Now press start. When you finish, turn off the machine. OK?
WOMAN: OK. Thanks a lot.
MAN: Anytime.

Exercise 4

Look at the schedule and listen to a part of the conversation.

EMPLOYEE: Excuse me, Mrs. Sims. What's my schedule for next week?
BOSS: Let's see, Jill. You'll work the day shift on Monday. Eight to four. OK?
EMPLOYEE: Yes, that's fine.
BOSS: And, uh, Tuesday, can you work the afternoon shift?
EMPLOYEE: Noon to eight?
BOSS: Uh-huh.
EMPLOYEE: Yes, that's OK next week.

Now listen again and complete the schedule.

EMPLOYEE: Excuse me, Mrs. Sims. What's my schedule for next week?
BOSS: Let's see, Jill. You'll work the day shift on Monday. Eight to four. OK?
EMPLOYEE: Yes, that's fine.
BOSS: And, uh, Tuesday, can you work the afternoon shift?
EMPLOYEE: Noon to eight?
BOSS: Uh-huh.
EMPLOYEE: Yes, that's OK next week.
BOSS: On Wednesday, you'll work the day shift again.
EMPLOYEE: All right.
BOSS: And let's see. On Thursday and Friday the night shift. Four to midnight. Is that OK?
EMPLOYEE: Yes.
BOSS: Can you work on the weekend?
EMPLOYEE: Only Saturday. And I prefer the afternoon shift.
BOSS: Fine. You can start at noon on Saturday.
EMPLOYEE: Thanks, Mrs. Sims.

Exercise 5

Can you predict what the person will say? Listen and circle the response.

1. Can you work the day shift next Saturday?
2. Excuse me. Can you show me how to insert this paper?
3. OK. Thanks for your help.
4. Excuse me. Are you busy right now?
5. Can you please show me how to use this machine?
6. Can you work the afternoon shift on Wednesday and Thursday?

UNIT 9

What seems to be the matter?

Look at the pictures and listen.

DOCTOR: Hello, Ms. Adams? Come on in. What seems to be the matter?
PATIENT: Well, doctor, I'm not sure.

1. PATIENT: I have this bad cold.
   DOCTOR: Oh, bless you!
   PATIENT: Uh, thanks.

2. PATIENT: And I have this bad cough, too!
   DOCTOR: Uh-huh. How long have you had the cough?
   PATIENT: Mmm, three days—since Friday.
   DOCTOR: Let's take a look. Breathe deeply.

3. DOCTOR: OK. Let me write you a prescription. Take one teaspoon every four hours. And call me next week. I hope you feel better soon!
   PATIENT: Thanks, doctor.

4. DOCTOR: Hi, Mr. King. What's the matter?
   PATIENT: Oh, doctor, I've got a terrible stomachache! I think it's the flu.
   DOCTOR: How long have you had the stomachache?
   PATIENT: Since yesterday.
   DOCTOR: OK. Let's have a look.

5. DOCTOR: Hello, Ms. Frank. What can I do for you?
   PATIENT: Well, doctor, I have a very bad headache.

6. PATIENT: And a fever.
   DOCTOR: All right. First, let's take your temperature.

Now look at the pictures again and listen.

(Repetition of above)

Exercise 1

Listen to the conversations. Match the conversations with the pictures.

1. DOCTOR: Hello, Ms. Frank. What can I do for you?
   PATIENT: Well, doctor, I have a bad headache.
2. DOCTOR: Here's your prescription. I hope you feel better soon.
   PATIENT: Thank you, doctor.
3. DOCTOR: What's the matter?
   PATIENT: I've got a very bad stomachache, doctor!
4. PATIENT: I think I have a fever.
   DOCTOR: Let's take your temperature.
5. DOCTOR: What seems to be the matter?
   PATIENT: I have a terrible cold.
6. DOCTOR: That's a bad cough.
   PATIENT: Yes. I've had it a few days.

Exercise 2

Number the sentences as you hear them.

DOCTOR: Hello, Ms. Adams? Come on in. What seems to be the matter?
PATIENT: I have this bad cold. And I have this bad cough, too.
DOCTOR: Let me write you a prescription. I hope you'll feel better.
DOCTOR: Hi, Mr. King. What's the matter?
PATIENT: I've got a terrible stomachache. I think it's the flu.
DOCTOR: Hello, Ms. Frank. What can I do for you?
PATIENT: Well, doctor, I have a very bad headache and a fever.
DOCTOR: Let's take your temperature.

Exercise 3

Listen and check the sentence you hear.

1. You've got the flu.
2. I have a terrible cold.
3. I have a very bad headache.
4. I've got a cough and a fever.
5. Let me take your temperature.

Exercise 4

Look at the pictures and listen.

1. A: Hello. Crown Manufacturing.
   B: Hello, Mrs. Brown? This is Lynn King. I'm afraid I can't make it to work today.
   A: Oh, what's the matter?
   B: I have an earache and a bad sore throat.
   A: Oh, I'm sorry. I hope you feel better soon.
   B: Thanks, Mrs. Brown. Bye.
   A: Goodbye.

2. A: Hello.
   B: Hi, Mr. Santos? This is Jack Waters. I'm sorry I can't come to work this week. I had a car accident.
   A: Oh, not serious, I hope! Are you all right?
   B: Well, yes. But I hurt my neck, and my leg and foot. And I have a very bad backache.
   A: I'm sorry, Jack. I hope you feel better soon.
   B: Thanks a lot, Mr. Santos. Bye.
   A: Bye, Jack.

Now listen again and number the words as you hear them.

(*Repetition of above*)

Exercise 5

Number the parts of the body as you hear them.

1. Stomach
2. Head
3. Back
4. Neck
5. Ear
6. Foot
7. Throat
8. Leg

Exercise 6

Listen and check what is wrong with the person in each conversation.

1. PATIENT: Hello, Dr. Franco.
   DOCTOR: Well, what seems to be the matter.
   PATIENT: I have a very sore throat.
   DOCTOR: Any fever?
   PATIENT: No, I don't think so.
   DOCTOR: Do you have an earache?
   PATIENT: Yes. And I've had a bad headache for two days.
   DOCTOR: OK. Let's check your throat first.

2. OPERATOR: Police Operator 33. Where's the emergency?

MAN: The corner of Fifth and Lake, in Newton.
OPERATOR: Yes?
MAN: We need an ambulance. A man fell and hurt his back and leg.
OPERATOR: OK. Don't move him. We'll be right there.

3. BOSS: Hello, Marshall's.
   EMPLOYEE: Hi, Mrs. Brodsky? This is Dennis Wade. I can't make it to work today. I had a little accident yesterday.
   BOSS: Oh, that's too bad!
   EMPLOYEE: I hurt my neck and I have a bad backache.
   BOSS: Oh, I hope you feel better soon, Dennis.
   EMPLOYEE: Thanks a lot. Bye.
   BOSS: Goodbye.

4. DOCTOR: How are you, Mr. Johnson?
   PATIENT: I feel sick, doctor.
   DOCTOR: What's wrong?
   PATIENT: I have a bad stomachache and a slight sore throat.
   DOCTOR: Hmm, any headaches?
   PATIENT: Yes, I have a headache, now.
   DOCTOR: Let me take your temperature.

UNIT 10

Mr. Meyers, we've got problems!

Look at the pictures and listen.

TENANT: Mr. Meyers, we've got problems!
LANDLORD: What's wrong?
TENANT: A lot of things. Please come in.

1. TENANT: Look! The lock is broken.
   LANDLORD: Hmm . . .

2. TENANT: The paint in here is peeling, too.
   LANDLORD: Uh-huh.

3. TENANT: This window is cracked.
   LANDLORD: Let's see.

4. TENANT: And the faucet leaks.
   LANDLORD: Oh, dear.

5. TENANT: And in the bathroom, the bathtub is clogged.
   LANDLORD: Uh-huh.

6. TENANT: And this outlet doesn't work.
   LANDLORD: Yeah. I'll take care of it.
   TENANT: When?
   LANDLORD: Tomorrow. I'll send someone tomorrow.
   TENANT: Morning?
   LANDLORD: Oh, yeah. Probably late morning.
   TENANT: OK. Good. I'll be here. Thanks, Mr. Meyers!

Now look at the pictures again and listen.

(*Repetition of above*)

Exercise 1

Listen to the conversations. Match the conversations with the pictures.

1. TENANT: Mr. Meyers, we've got problems!
   LANDLORD: What's the matter?
   TENANT: Look. The paint is peeling.
   LANDLORD: Hmm. Yeah . . .

2. TENANT: And in the bathroom, the outlet doesn't work.
   LANDLORD: OK. I'll take care of it.

3. LANDLORD: And what's wrong here?
   TENANT: Uh, the bathtub is clogged.
   LANDLORD: Hmm.

4. TENANT: Oh, and Mr. Meyers, the faucet leaks, too.
   LANDLORD: Let's see.

5. TENANT: Come in here. The window is cracked!
   LANDLORD: Yeah, I see. I'll take care of it.

6. LANDLORD: And what's the problem here?
   TENANT: The lock is broken.
   LANDLORD: Well, I'll send someone tomorrow.
   TENANT: Great. Thanks a lot.

Exercise 2

Number the sentences as you hear them.

TENANT: Mr. Meyers, we've got problems!
LANDLORD: What's wrong?
TENANT: Look! The lock is broken.
TENANT: The paint in here is peeling, too.
TENANT: The kitchen window is cracked.
LANDLORD: Let's see.
TENANT: And the faucet leaks. And in the bathroom, the bathtub is clogged.
TENANT: And this outlet doesn't work.
LANDLORD: Yeah. I'll take care of it.

Exercise 3

Look at the picture and listen.

1. LANDLORD: Hello?
   TENANT: Hello, Mr. Diaz?
   LANDLORD: Yes?
   TENANT: Mr. Diaz, this is Mrs. Fein from apartment 17. We need some work done in the apartment.
   LANDLORD: What's wrong?
   TENANT: Well, the light fixture is broken.

2. TENANT: The intercom doesn't work.

3. TENANT: And the mirror is cracked.

4. LANDLORD: Is that it?
   TENANT: No, the radiator leaks.
   LANDLORD: Hmm . . .

5. TENANT: The toilet leaks, too.
   LANDLORD: Oh, dear.

6. TENANT: And the sink is plugged up.
   LANDLORD: OK. I'll send someone tomorrow.
   TENANT: When?
   LANDLORD: Afternoon. Around two o'clock.

TENANT: OK. I'll be here. Thanks, Mr. Diaz. Bye.
LANDLORD: Bye.

Now listen again and repeat the sentences.

(*Repetition of above*)

Exercise 4

Listen and check the items you hear in each conversation.

1. TENANT: Oh, Mr. Meyers!
   LANDLORD: What is it, Mrs. Gold?
   TENANT: Our intercom doesn't work.
   LANDLORD: Hm.
   TENANT: And the bathtub is plugged up. The sink is cracked, too.
   LANDLORD: OK. I'll send someone first thing Monday.
   TENANT: Very good. Thank you!

2. TENANT: Excuse me, Mr. Meyers!
   LANDLORD: Yes, Mr. Wu?
   TENANT: We need some work done in the apartment.
   LANDLORD: What's wrong?
   TENANT: Please come in. The paint in here is peeling. Look!
   LANDLORD: Yes, I see.
   TENANT: And this outlet doesn't work.
   LANDLORD: Hmm . . .
   TENANT: In the bathroom, the radiator leaks. Oh, and this window is cracked.
   LANDLORD: I'll send someone soon.
   TENANT: When?
   LANDLORD: Monday afternoon. OK?
   TENANT: Great. Thanks, Mr. Meyers.

3. TENANT: Hello, Mr. Meyers.
   LANDLORD: Hello, Ms. Mills. How are you today?
   TENANT: Fine, thanks. You?
   LANDLORD: All right.
   TENANT: Oh, Mr. Meyers, we've got a few problems in the apartment.
   LANDLORD: What's the matter?
   TENANT: Well, the light fixture is broken. And the toilet leaks.
   LANDLORD: OK, Ms. Mills. I'll take care of it!
   TENANT: Can you send someone tomorrow?
   LANDLORD: No.
   TENANT: When?
   LANDLORD: Monday morning.
   TENANT: OK. Oh! This lock is broken, too.
   LANDLORD: Yes, I see. We'll take care of it.
   TENANT: Thanks, Mr. Meyers. I'll expect someone Monday.

ANSWER KEY

UNIT 1

What do we need?

Exercise 1: **a.** 5 **b.** 4 **c.** 7 **d.** 1 **e.** 2 **f.** 3 **g.** 6 **h.** 8
Exercise 2: **a.** 10 **b.** 6 **c.** 3 **d.** 9 **e.** 1 **f.** 8 **g.** 2
  h. 5 **i.** 4 **j.** 7 **k.** 11
Exercise 3: **1.** milk, eggs **2.** cooking oil **3.** cereal,
  bread **4.** laundry detergent, milk, flour **5.** bread,
  oil, flour **6.** eggs, cookies
Exercise 4: **a.** 4 **b.** 5 **c.** 1 **d.** 6 **e.** 3 **f.** 3
Exercise 5: **1.** are **2.** is **3.** is **4.** are **5.** are **6.** is
Exercise 6: **1.** h, k **2.** b, j **3.** i, k **4.** a, c, k, l
  5. b, d, e, f, g, j, l

UNIT 2

How much is this first class?

Exercise 1: **1.** a **2.** b **3.** d **4.** c **5.** b **6.** d
Exercise 2: **a.** 2 **b.** 9 **c.** 1 **d.** 7 **e.** 8 **f.** 3 **g.** 10
  h. 5 **i.** 4 **j.** 6
Exercise 3: **1.** c **2.** a **3.** b **4.** a **5.** c
Exercise 4: **1.** $3.00 **2.** $5.00 **3.** $10.75 **4.** 75¢
Exercise 5: **1.** a: 3, b: 2, e: 2, h: 1 **2.** a: 20, c: 10, f: 5,
  g: 5 **3.** d: 15, g: 2, h: 2 **4.** a: 10, b: 2, e: 3, f: 1

UNIT 3

Four pounds of apples, please.

Exercise 1: d, e, f, g
Exercise 2: b, c, e, g
Exercise 3: **a.** 6 **b.** 7 **c.** 1 **d.** 9 **e.** 5 **f.** 3 **g.** 2 **h.** 4
  i. 8
Exercise 4: **1.** head **2.** bunch **3.** pounds **4.** apples
  5. cheese **6.** half
Exercise 5: **a.** 2 **b.** 6 **c.** 3 **d.** 1 **e.** 5 **f.** 4
Exercise 6: **1.** a: ¼ pound, k: 1 box **2.** c: 5 pounds,
  g: 3 pounds, k: 1 box **3.** f: 3 bunches, i: ½ pound,
  j: 2 pounds **4.** a: ½ pound, b: 1 head, h: 2 pounds,
  i: 2 bunches **5.** d: 2 dozen, e: 3 pounds, f: 1 bunch,
  k: 3 boxes

UNIT 4

Do you have white semi-gloss paint?

Exercise 1: **1.** a **2.** c **3.** c, d **4.** b, c **5.** a, b **6.** b, c
  7. a, c
Exercise 2: **a.** 2 **b.** 7 **c.** 1 **d.** 9 **e.** 6 **f.** 3 **g.** 8 **h.** 5
  i. 4 **j.** 10
Exercise 3: **1.** paint, paintbrush **2.** hooks, sizes
  3. two, batteries **4.** quart, paint **5.** batteries
  6. large, hooks
Exercise 4: **1.** a: 2, b: 3, c: 1 **2.** a: 1, b: 2, c: 3 **3.** a: 4,
  b: 1, c: 3, d: 2
Exercise 5: **1.** c, f: 10 feet, k: wide **2.** a: quart, g: 100-
  watt, j: small **3.** a: gallon, b: small, e: wide, g: 60-
  watt, g: 100-watt **4.** d, h, i, k: narrow

UNIT 5

Do you want a ride home?

Exercise 1: **1.** a **2.** a **3.** b **4.** b **5.** b **6.** b **7.** a
Exercise 2: **a.** 3 **b.** 4 **c.** 10 **d.** 1 **e.** 2 **f.** 5 **g.** 8
  h. 6 **i.** 7 **j.** 9
Exercise 3: **1.** b **2.** a **3.** b **4.** a **5.** b
Exercise 4:

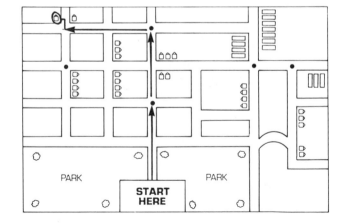

Exercise 5:
  1.